"This is good advice. Anybody can
evenings for dropping to the pres
what is deepest and best in onesel
and regularly, those five minutes v
you in more ways than you can imagine."

"The real gift lyi unwind from the day &   e
surprising discove make the most of your   it from
small daily investments. Brantley and Millstine's gentle,
engaging exercises lead the reader effortlessly into a daily
rhythm of reconnection and mindfulness. The resulting
sense of purposefulness and balance is priceless. This is a
book you'll feel compelled to share with friends and loved
ones alike."

—Dana Landis, Ph.D., life coach

in private practice

Jeffrey Brantley, MD
Wendy Millstine, NC

five
good
minutes
in the evening

**100 mindful practices to help you unwind
from the day & make the most of your night**

New Harbinger Publications, Inc.

Publisher's Note

This publication is designed to provide accurate and authoritative information in regard to the subject matter covered. It is sold with the understanding that the publisher is not engaged in rendering psychological, financial, legal, or other professional services. If expert assistance or counseling is needed, the services of a competent professional should be sought.

Distributed in Canada by Raincoast Books.

Copyright © 2006 by Jeffrey Brantley and Wendy Millstine
New Harbinger Publications, Inc.; 5674 Shattuck Avenue; Oakland, CA 94609
www.newharbinger.com

Second in the Five Good Minutes™ series

Five Good Minutes is a trademark of New Harbinger Publications, Inc.

Cover design by Amy Shoup; Text design by Amy Shoup and Michele Waters-Kermes
Acquired by Tesilya Hanauer; Edited by Jasmine Star

Library of Congress Cataloging-in-Publication Data

Brantley, Jeffrey.
  Five good minutes in the evening : 100 mindful practices to help you unwind from the day and make the most of your night / Jeffrey Brantley and Wendy Millstine.
       p. cm.
  ISBN-13: 978-1-57224-455-9
  ISBN-10: 1-57224-455-0
 1. Meditation. 2. Attention. 3. Imagery (Psychology) 4. Visualization. 5. Self-actualization (Psychology) I. Matik, Wendy-O, 1966- II. Title.
  BF637.M4B726 2006
  158.1'2—dc22

                          2006014693

08 07 06   10 9 8 7 6 5 4 3 2

This book is dedicated to all those whose labor and generosity help to make our world a better place. May you be safe and filled with peace. May you be happy and lighthearted.

—J.B.

For my sister, Nancy, whose gentle heart, generous spirit, and patience infuse every page.

—W.M.

contents

enriching your home life   89

introduction

Imagine living with a deeper sense of peace and calm and feeling more present and connected with loved ones and the richness of life, night or day.

How could you do it? Where would you start?

In our previous book, *Five Good Minutes: 100 Morning Practices to Help You Stay Calm and Focused All Day Long*, we invited you to explore the possibility that living your life in the present moment, wholeheartedly and with intention, can be radically transforming. Although five minutes of clock time can seem insignificant, the present moment—the eternal now—is enormously potent, and is, in fact, where life happens.

In our earlier book, we focused on brief practices for presence, wisdom, connection, joy, and ease aimed at the morning, a time of day when energy is expansive and the demands of the day are ahead of you. In this book, we offer 100 simple, five-minute practices for evening, a time for embracing different dimensions of life, relaxing, connecting with loved ones, and getting needed rest and renewal.

The five good minutes approach offers even the busiest person a precious opportunity to be in a different relationship with their own life. Each mindful breath is an opportunity to feel the life in and around you. Each moment, inhabited consciously, is a chance to discover your own greatness of heart, and to allow life to move you deeply.

The five good minutes concept is simple: take the time, for just five minutes, to be present mindfully, to set a clear intention, and to act wholeheartedly, without attachment to any outcome as you engage in a focused practice or activity. When you practice these skills—mindful presence, clear intention, and wholehearted action—the door opens for an immediate and rich experience in the present moment. Throughout this book, you'll find practices that direct you to breathe or listen mindfully for about a minute, then set your intention, then act wholeheartedly.

If you've never practiced mindfulness before, don't worry! In part 1 of this book, you'll find clear and easy-to-follow instructions for practicing mindful breathing and mindful listening. Refer back to these instructions as often as necessary. With practice, you'll discover the naturalness and ease of being present through mindful breathing or mindful listening. And if you begin to sense a power in these methods of being mindful that goes beyond five good minutes, be prepared to enjoy that, as well.

Done mindfully and wholeheartedly, each of the practices offers you a new way of experiencing yourself and your life and can give you insight and understanding. This can carry over to profound and rewarding changes grounded in being more present, feeling more connected, and opening more to the mystery and awe of life in these human bodies.

It's easy to become pulled out of ourselves when we're caught in the momentum of a busy workaday life and identified with what we think is so important. But the costs of such hijacking are high: worry and hurry may dominate your inner life; you may feel out of touch with loved ones and perhaps even a good night's sleep is no longer possible.

This book, like our previous one, is dedicated to helping you find and reclaim what is yours: a deeper and richer sense of joy, peace, connection, and meaning in the midst of the busyness and demands of your everyday work, home, and personal life.

Because the demands of the working world can be so intense, this book is focused on practices to help you let go of the momentum and aftereffects of your workday and inhabit more fully the larger landscape of your life. Living large in this way includes having fun, relaxing, and paying closer attention to your own inner life and the lives of those you love. We've also included a section of practices designed to help you get the rest you need and a good night's sleep.

In five short minutes a day, or even just a few times each week, the practices in this book can help you, or someone you love, reconnect with life in all of these ways:

- You'll feel more at ease and alive, and be more present for your life beyond the workaday world.

- You'll feel more in touch with your inner life, and enjoy more rewarding relationships with loved ones, including your pets.

- You'll explore more of the mystery and awe of this human life.

- You'll feel more calm and at peace, and hopefully get a good night's sleep.

PART 1

the foundation

Being There for the Gifts of Your Life

Five minutes is just clock time. The practices and activities in this book invite you to dwell in the present moment, which is always here and is timeless.

The experiences of life flow constantly into and out of the present moment. Conditions are always changing. In the morning, energy, thoughts, plans, and people are one way. By evening, everything can be totally different: energy levels change, echoes of the day can cloud your connection to your home and personal life, and doubts or worry may be dominating your inner life.

To embrace the wholeness of life and be available for all the gifts life offers you, it's important to learn to stay present and work with these changing conditions, whatever they are. The practices in this book are aimed at helping you make the transition from your workday and supporting you to be available for your life after work and into the evening, including getting the rest and sleep you need.

The present moment becomes a place you can inhabit more fully when you practice mindfulness—paying attention on purpose, as if it really mattered, to experiences happening both inside and outside your skin. The way you pay attention is important. Being mindful means paying attention in a welcoming, nonjudging way that seeks to understand and receive experience, not to change it. As human beings, we all have the ability to be mindful; we just have to know that and do it.

Being mindful can initiate a change in your relationship to your inner life that will ultimately allow you more freedom from the momentum and agitation that naturally arise in the course of a busy day. It can free you from habitual energy patterns, in both mind and body, and make you more available for action in the present moment.

Why Five Good Minutes in the Evening?

Do you ever feel as though you're living on a treadmill? Though the situations and context of life generally change in the evening, how often do events of the day echo in, or even distort, the evening's activities? Perhaps you've experienced some of these repercussions:

- Your body has left work, but your mind has not.

- Your physical energy is low, but hurry and worry are driving your thoughts.

- A friend speaks to you, but your attention is in the past or the future.

- At home, the dog brings a tug toy, the cat purrs, your child or partner touches your hand, but you're not present as this precious moment of life unfolds.

What has happened in these and countless other examples of absence and inattention? You've been hijacked by the momentum of a day full of thoughts, intentions, and actions. When you're replaying scenes, obsessing over plans, or beset by feelings of tension and worry, you're at risk of losing the promise of the evening, including rest and renewal.

Each five-minute practice in this book is a relaxing, fun, enriching, and creative opportunity to explore and experiment with a different way of being in, and relating to, your life as it changes from day into evening. Beyond facilitating that transition, you may well find that these practices help you develop a deeper sense of interconnection with others, and help you discover the greatness and mystery in the human heart.

How to Use This Book

The 100 practices in this book offer specific means for relaxing and releasing your workday, for enjoying your home life and your time with loved ones and pets, and for supporting you in getting a good night's sleep.

You don't have to do all 100 of them.

You don't have to like or enjoy all 100 of them.

You don't have to work through them in sequence, from 1 to 100.

What is helpful is to approach each practice in the spirit of relaxing and having fun. Try to take the attitude that the practice is there as a friend or ally, to aid and comfort you. These practices won't be as helpful if you make them just another chore on your already overloaded to-do list.

Read through the practices any way you like and look for practices that appeal to you. Those that sound like fun, that evoke a sense of relief inside you just by reading them, or that stimulate your sense of curiosity are the best ones to start with. Be aware that which practices seem appealing may vary from day to day or over time, so it's good to go back and review different and untried practices from time to time.

Being patient with yourself is very important. From our point of view, you *cannot* make a mistake doing any practice as long as you're willing to make an honest effort. As we point out in the section on acting wholeheartedly, doing the practice without attachment to outcome is very helpful. In other words, just do it and see what happens without putting any extra pressure on the practice or yourself to "make it work."

You'll probably find it helpful to read the description a couple of times or so before actually doing the practice. Alternatively, you could ask someone to read it aloud or you could record the instructions yourself.

You may also want to explore sharing a practice with your partner, a child, or a group of friends or colleagues. In this case, everyone does the practice at the same time while one person reads it or while listening to a recorded version of the instructions. It can be very rewarding to spend some time afterward sharing and discussing each person's experience.

Finally, when you find practices you like, don't feel you have to limit yourself to only five minutes, only in the evening, or only once a day! Explore and enjoy working with your favorite practices as much as you like.

It All Begins with Being Present

Life is happening in this moment, and the richness of life becomes available only when you are present for it. Establishing your attention in the present moment is the first minute of your five good minutes (whether the practice instruction says so explicitly or not). Anything you do becomes more rich and potent when you take a minute or so to establish your attention and awareness in the present moment before doing anything else.

Being present includes feeling a sense of peace and ease. We've included practices to help you relax, release stress and tension, and even laugh. You may wish to find one of these and spend your five good minutes relaxing and releasing tension. It can be a good use of your time!

Being present requires that you make the effort to be here, in the present moment, by paying attention. In this book, you'll find practices to help you focus your attention mindfully so that you can connect more fully with each moment of your life, including the five good minutes. As you do more and more mindful practice, your mindfulness will brighten and your access to the present moment will increase.

Being present includes being patient when your attention wanders away. This happens to everyone. Kindness and patience with yourself will support you as you bring your attention back, time and again—even in a short five minutes.

Being present happens more easily when you let go of any thoughts about the *next* anything, and connect instead with *this* breath in *this* moment. You may not be able to be present for five breaths or ten sounds, but you can be present for *this* breath or *this* sound.

Your Keys to Being Present

It takes some skill and practice to be truly present. In this book, we refer to this way of being present as "being mindful," and by that we mean paying attention on purpose in a friendly and nonjudging way that allows experience to come to you.

When you pay attention mindfully, you don't seek to change, add, or subtract anything from what you're experiencing. It is actually a practice just to be mindful. You practice paying attention—as if it really mattered—to your experience in this moment, as it unfolds, and as you allow yourself to receive whatever arises.

There are many ways to establish mindfulness. They all depend on paying attention on purpose, as if it really mattered, without judgment, and without trying to change anything about the experience you're observing. You'll find many different ways to be mindful in the practices throughout this book.

There are two types of mindfulness practice that are so helpful and important that they deserve special mention: mindful breathing and mindful listening. Each method offers you a way to inhabit the present moment more fully, and either can be the first step of your five good minutes.

In this book and our previous one, many of the exercises actually begin with the words "Breathe mindfully for about a minute." Mindful breathing is an ancient and powerful way to establish your awareness in the present moment. Below, you'll find some simple instructions to guide you in practicing mindful breathing. However, mindful breathing may not always be easy, so we've also provided instructions for mindful listening, wherein you focus your attention on sounds in your environment

When might you choose one method over the other? Many people find that it's difficult to concentrate attention on the breath when their minds are racing or very busy. Or they may be distracted from their breath by the sounds around them when they're in a noisy situation. To ensure you can practice even in such situations, you may want to work on mindfully listening to the sounds themselves. Mindful listening tends to help you access a sense of inner spaciousness that can more easily include all that is happening, even distractions. Alternatively, if you're feeling spaced-out or out of touch with your body, or if you're feeling restless and agitated, concentrating attention on the narrow focus of your breath sensations can be just the thing to bring you into the present moment with a sense of stillness and calm.

Mindful Breathing and Mindful Listening: The First Element of Your Five Good Minutes

Below are easy-to-follow instructions for practicing mindful breathing and mindful listening. Experiment and have fun with both. Return to these instructions as often as needed to make your mindfulness practice strong. The more confident you feel with each of these methods of practicing mindfulness, the more likely you are to use them, not only in specific five-minute practices, but also in other situations where added presence and awareness are valuable elements of your total experience.

In essence, mindful breathing is simply directing your attention entirely to a focus on your breath—observing it as it occurs without attempting to control it. Here are some simple instructions for mindful breathing:

① Make yourself comfortable. You can do mindful breathing in any posture: sitting, lying down, standing, or even walking.

② To reduce distractions, close your eyes or focus softly on a spot on the ground a few feet ahead of you.

③ For the time of this practice, let go of all agendas. You don't have to become anyone or anything else or make anything special happen. You already have what it takes to be mindful. Just relax.

④ Gently bring your attention to your body, and then to the sensations of your breath moving in your body. Rest your attention at the spot where it is easiest for you to actually feel your breath moving in and out. The chest or abdomen rising and falling or the tip of the nose are common points of focus.

⑤ Let the breath sensations come to you. You need not control your breath in any way. Let it flow naturally as you bring a kind, allowing attention to the sensations of inhaling, pausing, exhaling, and so on, breath after breath.

⑥ When your attention wanders away from your breath, you haven't made a mistake or done anything wrong. Simply notice this movement of attention, understanding it as a habit of your mind, and kindly return your attention to the breath sensations happening in the moment. Your mind will likely move away from your breath countless times. Each time, just notice where it went and practice kindness and patience with yourself as you return your attention to the breath sensations happening in the moment.

⑦ Don't struggle with being present for many or even a few breaths, but instead focus on connecting with *this breath*, this inhalation, this exhalation. Even if you can't focus on two consecutive breaths, you can focus on this breath. To be present for this breath is good enough.

⑧ Move your attention closer, noticing the quality of each new breath as accurately and continuously as you can. Try to stay present for the entire cycle of the breath: in, pause, out, pause.

⑨ End your breath meditation by shifting your focus off of your breath sensations, opening your eyes, and moving gently.

In addition to breathing mindfully, it's often useful, especially when you wish to calm yourself or relax, to deliberately breathe deeply, from your abdomen, not just your chest. Some of the practices will instruct you to breathe deeply or *diaphragmatically*. By that we mean deepening your breath so that your diaphragm (the muscle that separates your chest and abdomen) expands downward, and your belly rises.

To check how you're breathing, place one hand on your chest and the other on your belly, above your navel. Which hand moves more as you breathe? To ensure that you're breathing diaphragmatically, work on expanding your diaphragm downward (taking a deeper breath). This will cause the hand on your belly to move more than the hand on your chest. While it's possible to breathe adequately by simply expanding and contracting your chest, diaphragmatic breathing—deep belly breathing—is a powerful tool for inducing calm and even relieving anxiety. Next time you're overtaken by a strong negative emotion, give diaphragmatic breathing a try and see how it affects you.

Here are some important things to remember about mindful breathing and diaphragmatic breathing, and some distinctions between them:

- Deep, diaphragmatic breathing requires conscious effort beyond the body's natural breathing.

- By deliberately involving your diaphragm in breathing, you are breathing more deeply, from your abdomen, and you can help your body take in more oxygen. When people are anxious or stressed, they often fall into habits of shallow, rapid breathing that involve moving the chest but not the abdomen. By deliberately breathing from your abdomen, you can shift out of these habits of shallow breathing and poor oxygenation in times of anxiety or stress.

- Diaphragmatic breathing is a powerful practice for moving more breath into and out of the body. You only need to take a few of these intentionally deeper breaths when practicing this form of breathing. Your body rarely needs such a large volume of air in each breath for a prolonged period. As you begin to feel the benefits of a few deeper breaths, and perhaps a sense of calm arising, let go of the diaphragmatic breathing and allow your body to breathe naturally, at its own depth and rhythm.

- "Breathing mindfully"—as we are using the phrase in this book—is practiced by paying attention to sensations arising from the body's natural breathing patterns. Mindful breathing doesn't require any control of the breathing process.

- And, of course, you can be "mindful" of diaphragmatic breathing.

Mindful listening involves directing your attention entirely to a focus on the sounds in your environment, whatever they may be. Simply receive and observe them without labeling or judging them. Here are some simple instructions for mindful listening:

①   Make yourself comfortable. You can do mindful listening in any posture: sitting, lying down, standing, or even walking.

②   To reduce distractions, close your eyes or focus softly on a spot on the ground a few feet ahead of you.

③   For the time of this practice, let go of all agendas. You don't have to become anyone or anything else or make anything special happen. You already have what it takes to be mindful. Just relax.

④   Focus your attention on the sounds around you.

⑤   Let the sounds come to you, receiving each without preference.

⑥ Let go of any thoughts about the sounds; instead, focus on the direct experience of sound itself.

⑦ Allow your focus to deepen to include all sounds.

⑧ Listen and receive, allowing one sound, then another. Notice how one sound fades and is replaced by another. Notice even the space between the sounds. Relax, soften, and open.

⑨ Let the meditation support you. Listen and open as sounds come and go. Rest in the stillness that receives all sounds.

⑩ End your meditation by shifting your focus from the sounds, opening your eyes, and moving gently.

Intention: The Second Element of Your Five Good Minutes

Setting a clear intention is a way of pointing yourself in the direction of an important value or goal. Intention precedes all movement in these human bodies, so it's good to learn to identify intention, and to practice setting wise intentions.

Setting intention can be done skillfully or unskillfully. For example, it wouldn't be very skillful to set an intention to be 100 percent worry free as a goal that must be achieved. Be careful not to set an intention that's unrealistic or that you must achieve at all costs. This is a setup for harsh self-criticism and possibly cynicism about being able to do anything to help yourself.

An intention arrived at skillfully is more like a friendly guide. It points you in the right direction but acknowledges that important changes can take time. Patience and kindness toward yourself as you move in your chosen direction are important allies on the journey. Your intention to be worry free, for example, may be better thought of as a direction you'd like to travel in. Since being entirely free of worries probably isn't realistic, setting a goal such as "to worry less and relax more" might be more practical.

Each of the 100 practices in this book has the potential to support whatever intention you might select. Through the simple act of making a statement of intention, you open the door to a profound shift in your life in the present moment.

Acting Wholeheartedly: The Final Piece of Your Five Good Minutes

As you do the practice you have chosen, you are encouraged to act wholeheartedly, without attachment to outcome. What does this mean? Acting wholeheartedly means doing something with all of your attention and energy. If you've established mindfulness and set your intention, you've already built a powerful support for wholehearted action.

You may find it takes some practice to be wholehearted, even for five minutes. Much of what we do in life is done without our full attention or commitment for a variety of reasons. These habits of inattention and disconnection can be overcome, but it may take some effort to do so.

So, as you begin to try the practices in the book, be patient and give yourself some room to grow. Also, notice how the different practices are more appropriate to different moods, times, and phases of your day and night.

Once you've selected practices that seem to fit, try nurturing a willingness to experiment, without demanding immediate results or a quick fix. If you get immediate results (it is possible!), be grateful. But you'll probably find it easier to be wholehearted while doing your practice if you let go of trying to change anything or make anything happen. This is what we mean when we say "without attachment to outcome." Just do the practice without vigilantly watching and judging what is happening.

It is perfectly okay if you feel awkward, silly, or embarrassed as you do your practice. Remember, you cannot make a mistake as long as you give it your best effort. So just acknowledge whatever you're feeling (that's a moment of mindfulness, by the way) and keep on doing it!

100 Doorways to Possibility

Life is filled with possibilities, if only we can see them and open to them. Habitual energy patterns block us from the richness of life, moment by moment, but you don't have to remain stuck in those patterns. There is another way beyond the one of inattention, contraction, and reactivity. Each time you take five good minutes, you open a doorway for engaging life freshly and opening to new possibilities.

So be practical, selecting practices that call to you and working with them patiently. Be gentle with yourself, allowing for your own wandering mind and any distractions that arise. And be willing to be playful, have some fun, and be surprised.

By taking advantage of the transforming and healing power of mindfulness, intention, and wholeheartedness, anywhere and anytime you choose, you gain direct access to the infinite possibilities in your life. May you inhabit your possibilities!

This book offers you 100 ways to begin. We hope you'll find joy, ease, awe, and empowerment through these practices.

PART 2

the practices

leaving work at work

1

relax and release the workday

When you're still at work and finishing your day, take five good minutes to leave all of your work at work.

① Sit comfortably and close your eyes.

② Breathe mindfully or listen mindfully for about a minute.

③ Set your intention. For example, "May this practice enable me to leave work and feel finished, in heart, mind, and body."

④ Continue mindful breathing or listening and allow yourself to release tensions, softening and opening as much as feels safe to you.

⑤ Speaking quietly to yourself, acknowledge the end of your workday. Say something like "Now I am done with work" or "I'm leaving work now." Or use whatever phrase feels right to you.

⑥ Breathe mindfully for a few more breaths.

⑦ If you like, you could offer an aspiration or a prayer. For example, "May the highest good come from my work today."

⑧ End by opening your eyes and moving gently. ✳

2

clarity of vision

A strenuous workday can often lead to eyestrain and exhaustion. Sore, dry, and itchy eyes, a common complaint among computer users, can interfere with concentration and even interrupt sleep. We rely heavily on our sight to carry us through our endless tasks, yet we neglect to nurture our eyes. Before you leave work, take the next five minutes to reduce eye discomfort.

① Begin by sitting down, closing your eyes, and taking a few deep, diaphragmatic breaths. Allow the tension to flow out of your body with each exhalation.

② Rest your fingertips along the lower edges of your eyebrows. Using a circular motion, massage the area with gentle pressure, always circling outward.

③ Move slowly around the outer perimeter of your eyes, along the edge of the bone that encircles your eyes. Remain at each spot for ten seconds, always circling outward.

④ End by dropping your arms to your sides.

Your eyes deserve a break. A simple eye massage can restore your vision and bring a sense of inner calm. ✳

3

float away

Stress and workday pressures can make your heart, mind, and body feel increasingly solid and heavy. When you feel this way, what would it be like to soften and open to spaciousness?

① Breathe or listen mindfully for about a minute.

② Set your intention. For example, "May this practice give me ease and lightness."

③ Bring your attention to the sensations inside your body. Acknowledge any sense of contraction, holding, or tension.

④ Breathe or listen mindfully.

⑤ Shift your attention to your thoughts and feelings. Acknowledge any worry, anxiety, or repeating thoughts.

⑥ Breathe or listen mindfully.

⑦ Imagine that your solid body softens, and that your heart, mind, and body flow together and expand into a beautiful balloon.

⑧ Let the balloon float up and away—as far and as high as feels safe.

⑨ Rest in spaciousness, ease, and lightness.

⑩ End by returning to the ground, now more relaxed. ✳

4

those nagging workday memories

Do you ever feel invaded by nagging memories of events from your day at work? If you have trouble getting those thoughts out of your head, try this practice.

① Whenever you notice thoughts or feelings about a work situation arising in the present moment, gently acknowledge them, saying something like "The story [or the thoughts] about work are here now."

② Anchor your awareness in the present moment by breathing mindfully or listening mindfully for about a minute.

③ Notice any deeper feelings beneath the thoughts, such as upset, worry, anger, or excitement. Name them kindly and allow them to be just as they are as you continue mindful breathing or listening.

④ As you name the thoughts or feelings, speak kindly to each one. Say something like "I release you" or "Thank you, but not now." You may have to speak to each one several times. Always speak kindly.

⑤ End by shifting your focus to your breath or to sounds and resting in the present moment as you open your eyes and move gently. ✳

5

wind down at the end of the workday

The last half hour at work is often a mad rush to pull together every last-minute task. You may find yourself frantically dashing in and out of your office, cubicle, or work area in a frenetic attempt to get this done or that tied up or that saved. If you structure your workday to end with stress, it leaves you stressed.

If you can reorganize your workload at the end of the day to reflect a slowing down of tasks, you'll begin to break the shackles of that frenzied pace. Toward the end of your work-day, take five good minutes to think about how you can adjust your tasks and pacing so that you wind down, instead of ending in a flurry of activity. Instead of finding more work or pressuring yourself to tie up all the loose ends, tell yourself that there is always tomorrow and that your pile of unfinished work can just wait. In the last half hour of your workday, try to cut back on the number of tasks you would normally tackle. Save simple and more pleasurable tasks for the end of the day so you can wind down. ✳

6

not only the expert

Mental habits of judgment and self-criticism can create a virtual prison wherein your work—no matter how successful— never seems good enough. If this is the case for you, it may lead to a tendency to feel like *you* aren't good enough, either. An identity (and a prison) can be created from the insatiable need to be more competent and more expert. What would it be like to *not* have to be so competent or so expert?

① Breathe or listen mindfully for about a minute.

② Set your intention. For example, "May this practice help me find balance in my life."

③ Breathe or listen mindfully for a few more breaths.

④ Quietly, in your heart and mind, ask a question such as "Who am I besides the information I manage and the skills I possess?" or "What am I besides the work I do?"

⑤ Listen for all the responses. Repeat the question if necessary.

⑥ If it helps, keep this question with you day and night. ✳

7

minimize the workload

How can we leave work at work? The endless details and computations can cling to our every thought. You may find yourself speaking your mental list aloud: "Remember to call human resources. Need new software program. E-mail staff about changing the time of the meeting next week." Some of us even take our work home, running errands for work-related projects or making work-related phone calls.

When you let work dominate your off hours, you forget how to leave work at the office. But a good balance between work and rest is vital to your happiness. Just as you let work overtake you, allow yourself to completely and wholeheartedly immerse yourself into your after-work relaxation time. Instead of waiting for the weekend to enjoy life, schedule fun or pleasurable things to do when your workday comes to a close, such as a massage, a pedicure, or dinner and a movie. ✳

8

watch your speed

Hurry and momentum from the workday is easily internalized and, like a rapid drumbeat, can dictate your inner tempo long after your workday ends. Near the end of your workday, experiment with shifting to a different tempo.

① Find a place that offers privacy.

② Breathe or listen mindfully for about a minute.

③ Set your intention. For example, "May this practice bring me ease and joy."

④ Bring attention to your mind and body. Are your thoughts racing? Is there tension anywhere in your body? Is either your mind or your body agitated?

⑤ Stand up and start consciously moving your body at a speed that matches your inner speed. Walk, shake, or move for about a minute, really feeling the sensations.

⑥ Now take another minute or two and slow down deliberately, gently, and consciously, until you are stopped. Sit down.

⑦ Relax and breathe mindfully.

⑧ End by moving out at your new speed. ✳

9

detox the negativity

Whether you like your job or not, few things are more stressful than toxic coworkers. These negative people can pollute a perfectly productive day and leave you drained and unhappy. Their depressing energy is contagious, and it's important to find ways to safeguard yourself from this gloom. The following practice will help you develop immunity to their toxicity.

① Find a place that offers privacy, whether you're still at the office, alone at the bus stop, or seated in your car. Start by taking some deep, expansive breaths.

② Clear this dark energy by giving yourself a detoxing pep talk. Begin by acknowledging how toxic people can affect your mood and destabilize your day.

③ Next, tap into the well of forgiveness that resides inside you and visualize freeing your anger or resentment toward these toxic people. Imagine that your loving-kindness could heal a part of what is hurting these broken people.

④ Say aloud to yourself, "I am a compassionate and caring person. I like most people. I can see their weaknesses and know that their behavior doesn't have to do with me. I am surrounded by kind and gentle people." ✳

10

dear friends and colleagues

Like all other relationships, workplace relationships involve some friction. Could your inner relationship to a coworker impact both of you?

This practice invites you to experiment with the inner relationship. Notice when this practice begins to affect the outer relationship.

① Breathe or listen mindfully for about a minute.

② Set your intention. For example, "May this practice strengthen my work relationships."

③ Think of someone you work with whom you like.

④ Imagine speaking to that person in a friendly way, wishing them well, saying "May you be happy," "May you be safe," or something similar.

⑤ Now think of someone you work with who is difficult.

⑥ Imagine speaking to this person in the same friendly way, using your kind words. You aren't excusing this person's bad behavior, you're just practicing friendliness.

⑦ End by being quiet. Notice, honor, and learn from all of your feelings and reactions to this practice. ✳

11

body refreshment

Have you ever noticed how the last hour of your workday can be the toughest? You may feel anxious about not having enough time to complete what's on your plate, or you may feel the treacherous nagging of each minute dragging by seemingly without end. In either case, you've likely stored up tension somewhere in your body. The following exercise will help you reconnect with your body and release its pockets of strain and fatigue.

① Find a comfortable and quiet place to stand and take a minute to breathe mindfully, focusing on feeling your lungs filling with air expansively and then emptying on the release.

② Take this time to identify where in your body you're experiencing tightness or pain. Do you trap your tension in your neck? Shoulders? Jaw? Lower back?

③ Depending on where you feel tension, from a standing position give that part of your body a decent stretch. For example, you may want to place your arms above your head, gradually lengthening and extending each arm toward the sky in an alternating left-right movement. Or try gently lowering your head toward your chest and returning to a normal position, then lowering your head slowly to your left shoulder and then your right shoulder, taking five seconds at each position. ✳

12

plan tomorrow today—
then leave it

The present moment is the only moment. By inhabiting this moment with greater awareness, you actually shape the moments that follow. This is the only way we have to influence the future: to inhabit and own the present.

Try planning mindfully for tomorrow's workday.

① Near the end of your workday, give yourself some privacy and sit quietly.

② Breathe or listen mindfully for about a minute.

③ Set your intention. For example, "May this practice bring ease to my work."

④ Look around your workspace.

⑤ Ask yourself, "What are the most important things for me to do here tomorrow?"

⑥ Write as many as five things that come to mind.

⑦ Breathe mindfully for a few breaths.

⑧ Ask "What should be the first thing?" Circle it.

⑨ Leave your list in a place where you can find it easily.

⑩ Leave all of your work and worries there, too. ✳

13

unravel yourself

Even if you aren't a person who takes your work home, you may find it difficult to decompress. Scurrying thoughts of work details and conversations may haunt you for hours after your workday ends. In the following mindful visualization, imagine that you're a spool of thread unraveling from the clutches of work-related stress.

① Take one minute to connect with your breathing and ground yourself in the present moment. You can do this at your desk, on the subway, or while walking home.

② With the first rotation of your spool of thread, you're unwinding your tiresome list of worries. You're freeing yourself from their grip on your life.

③ On the second spin of the spool, you're unraveling your burdensome thoughts about what you left undone at work. Tomorrow you'll have a chance to get to it; but for now, there is no room for work.

④ With each unraveling, you are loosening from your spiraling thoughts and returning to a place of restored serenity. ✳

14

endless errands

Even though you've clocked out of your day job, sometimes you still have fifty-five places you have to get to after work—the dry cleaners, the supermarket, day care, and so on. This inexhaustible list of errands can further exacerbate your stress level, and yet you cannot escape these tiresome duties. Here are some helpful tips for making the most of the week and keeping your stress at bay:

- At the beginning of the week, make a running list of the errands that are an absolute priority, such as picking up the kids, shopping for food, and returning library books and rented movies.

- Make a separate list of secondary errands that don't have such strict deadlines, such as purchasing clothes, dog treats, or items for the house. Give yourself permission to put off these less-demanding tasks until the weekend.

Prioritizing helps you organize your after-work drive more efficiently and distributes your errands more evenly. Hopefully you'll find yourself with fewer errands to run and more time for fun on the weekend. ✳

15

awards presentation

Judges in your own mind can dominate your inner life. They may say "not good enough" or "not enough" about many of the good things you do. However, these judges are only inner habits of criticism and hostility. They *can* be retired.

This practice will help you establish a different habit—appreciating and honoring yourself and your work.

① Give yourself some privacy and sit quietly.

② Breathe or listen mindfully for about a minute.

③ Set your intention. For example, "May this practice help me appreciate myself more."

④ Breathe mindfully for a few more breaths.

⑤ Recall a success or something positive you said or did during your day at work today. See how the good outcome depended on you and your unique gifts.

⑥ Picture giving yourself a beautiful award to acknowledge this good work. Your award includes a sincere thank-you or a warm congratulations.

⑦ Allow yourself to open, then step forward to receive your award graciously. ✳

16

the art of patience

Some of us are more patient about waiting in line than others. No matter where you fall on this spectrum, you will at some point unavoidably find yourself stuck in the longest grocery line with the slowest checkout clerk, who appears content to wait a seeming eternity for a price check that never comes. How can you unruffle your anxiety and cultivate a more relaxed attitude for the long wait ahead of you? The following coping exercise may only take the five minutes that you're stuck waiting for your number to be called.

①   Begin with taking three deep, slow breaths. On each inhalation, sense the vitality and life force of oxygen charging your body and blood. On each exhalation, be conscious of your ability to decompress and release the avalanche of stressors in front of you.

②   The first thing to acknowledge is that you have the power to change the way you cope with stress, both psychologically and physiologically. Say to yourself, "I'm feeling stressed right now, but I have the innate ability to accept my situation and find patience in this moment. The road to patience brings harmony."

③   No matter where you've buried your patience, imagine that merely saying the word "patience" will help guide you there instantly. You may even want to write the word on a piece of paper and keep it in your wallet as a reminder for those dire, stress-ridden moments. ✳

🌙 17

---

traveler, be well

Impatience, distraction, irritation—how often do these energies (and their kin) accompany you on the commute home? Arising from many sources, these unpleasant feelings upset your transition from work to home life and color your evening. Experiment with a different energy—friendliness—as you travel home.

① Traveling home, with your eyes open, breathe mindfully for about a minute.

② Set your intention. For example, "May this practice bring me balance and ease."

③ Notice those around you—in cars, on foot, in buses or trains.

④ Reflect how each of them, like you, has difficulties in their day and in their life.

⑤ Imagine speaking to each one as if they were a good friend and wish each well using a phrase like "May you be well," "May you be happy," or "May you be safe."

⑥ End by sitting silently for a few breaths. Notice what you feel. ✳

C 18

humor me, please

It may seem absurd to schedule in laughter on your to-do list, but there's a good chance you've fallen out of practice. Maybe there was nothing funny about work today and nothing funny about the news headlines. You may be hard-pressed to find laughter, and you're likely to be charged admission when you do discover it. Take the next few minutes to generate a mental or written list of what makes you giggle. Here are some ideas to get you going on your list of after-work destressors:

- Rent a comedy, even if you've already seen it; it's sure to stir a chuckle out of you.

- Watch a television program featuring bloopers or goofy behavior by animals or people.

- Call a friend who has a comedic outlook on life or who brings out your silly side.

- Find a Web site that offers jokes for the day and be sure to share it with a coworker or friend.

When stress accumulates, one small humorous or absurdly ridiculous moment can defuse the situation, help you move past it, or, at the very least, distract you long enough to diminish its effect on you. ✳

19

---

find your release valve

Even if you're not the one driving, commuting in a traffic jam is unbearable. It is likely one of the top ten life stressors in the U.S. Combine this frustration with being in a hurry, and you have a lethal dose of chronic aggravation. We face our greatest challenges to peace of mind under these demanding conditions, where the goal of inner peace may seem like a remote island with no inhabitants. But don't lose hope! You may not be able to change your circumstances, but you can have a quick and easy action plan for diffusing your stress.

- As traffic slows, exit routes evaporate, and your heart begins to race, take five slow, diaphragmatic breaths, training yourself to breathe stress away. With each exhalation, let your mind and body soften mildly without losing concentration on the traffic around you.

- The key to this exercise is to identify a release valve amidst the madness. Your release valve may involve finding an upbeat radio station and singing at the top of your lungs, listening to a book on tape, letting off some steam by screaming out loud in your car, or pulling off safely at an exit and calling a supportive friend or family member.

- Make a written list of these stress regulators and keep it in the glove compartment so you'll have it when you need it. ✳

20

total body check-in

Stress accumulates in your body throughout a busy work-day. Vulnerable areas like your neck, scalp, and shoulders can become more and more tense as the pressure builds. Try checking in with your body for a minute or two a few times a day. Off-load stress each time and leave work feeling more at ease at the end of your day.

① Take a minute or two to stop what you're doing and breathe or listen mindfully for a few breaths.

② Turn mindful attention to your body, especially the flow of sensations within your body.

③ Pay attention to any specific parts or areas that are calling out to you. Allow yourself to feel the sensations there as they are happening. Meet and receive each sensation with kindness.

④ Imagine that each exhalation carries away all unnecessary tension and that each inhalation brings calm and ease to any tense areas of your body.

⑤ Finish by opening your eyes and moving gently. ✳

21

mind walk

When you've had a workday particularly full of pressures, take a five-minute mindful walk inside your life before you race home or take on errands. This simple exercise will clear your mind and help you make a clean break from your pestering work irritations. In this mind walk, you'll travel inward, through your own mind, and slow down so you can really take a look at and acknowledge what you're thinking and feeling. Along your leisurely mental stroll, take notice of the details of what's bothering you, where you're at emotionally, and what brought you there:

- Do you feel disappointed, lacking in affection, or worried about your health?

- Did your day leave you drained, scattered, or disoriented?

- What creative activities can you arrange to help alleviate this weighty outlook?

When you slow down your pace, even for a few minutes, in order to take note of the ebb and flow of your feelings, you unlock the doorway to emotional healing and extraordinary insight, which all too often get pushed aside because of a hurried schedule. ✳

22

be a tourist—on the way home

It's easy to fall into habits of inattention, becoming unconscious to the wonder of life as it unfolds within the routines of daily life. Try something different. Give a new twist to something you do every day: Let your daily commute home from work become a time and place for connecting with and discovering the richness of life all around you.

① Pause for a few mindful breaths before leaving work.

② Set your intention. For example, "May this practice awaken me to the wonder of life."

③ Imagine that you're a tourist and haven't been in this place in years—perhaps never before. You're very interested in what's happening here!

④ As you travel home, see with fresh eyes that are interested and curious about each and every thing. See how many new and interesting things or people you can notice.

⑤ Relax and have some fun! ✳

23

get out of the rut

Agonizingly long workdays and mounting pressures from deadlines are enough to get you stuck in the rut of a mindless routine. However, it's vital to your health and well-being to expose yourself to new things. One time per week, try something that you've never done before or that you haven't done for a long time. Here are a couple of end-of-the-day ideas to get you started:

- Eat at a new restaurant.

- Take a dance class.

- Do something creative—paint, draw, or play music.

- Play miniature golf with a loved one.

- Check out some live music from a different culture.

- Visit your local farmers' market for today's freshest organic produce.

- Write a love letter to someone you don't even know.

Be creative in your search for things you've never tried before or that you've longed to get back into the habit of. A daily routine can become dangerously mind-numbing. Expose yourself to new activities and rejuvenate your adventurous side. ✳

24

inward focus

Most nine-to-fivers will agree that they need an hour after work to decompress, but they rarely find the time to do so. For the next week, take just five minutes every day to follow this simple inward focus meditation.

① Start with a few breaths, unhurried and deliberate, originating from your core. Each breath is a practice in releasing pent-up strain and work worries.

② This meditation requires you to concentrate on a single imaginary object, such as a blade of grass or a candle flame. Choose the object you'd like to focus on.

③ Once you have a clear picture of this object in your mind's eye, your thoughts and feelings will ebb and flow naturally, as they always do, but you'll continue to refocus on the object in your mind's eye. By doing so, you are repositioning your attention to the present moment, and this will help free you from distraction by worries, anxieties, and outside pressures. You may experience a flood of worries or a river of guilt for not being more productive, but it's important to be in the here and now and to give yourself permission to focus inward. Recognize that those outside concerns are not permanent, they don't define who you are, and they can't control your life unless you let them. ✳

25

wide-open space

When you're caught in the demands and pace of the day, it's easy to begin to feel painfully pressured and contracted within. The following practice can help you reconnect with your inner spaciousness and feelings of calm and ease.

① Shortly before leaving work, or shortly after arriving at home, sit comfortably where you won't be disturbed.

② Breathe or listen mindfully for about a minute.

③ Set your intention. For example, "May this practice help me feel spaciousness and ease."

④ Close your eyes and picture yourself sitting comfortably.

⑤ Expand your view, as if the camera were moving back slowly.

⑥ See yourself growing smaller. See your home, your town, your region growing smaller and smaller. Continue until you are viewing the earth itself from space.

⑦ Relax into the spaciousness. Enjoy the feelings of ease and release. Breathe mindfully, feeling inner calm and stillness.

⑧ End by opening your eyes and moving gently. Let spaciousness and calm support you. ✳

26

the homestretch

Imagine if your commute home from work could be like window shopping; each passing storefront, sidewalk, garden, car, and pedestrian would become a stroll through a museum. Visualize the freeway as an architectural monument and consider every building a structural splendor, eliciting awe and wonder. Take notice of every shrub or tree and imagine if we had a word for every shade of green. Your journey home is an opportunity to see the world as if for the first time. You may notice extraordinary things that you never saw before, such as a stained glass window, schoolchildren hugging, or a smile from a passing stranger.

After work, set your mind at ease and immerse yourself in the sights and sounds of your neighborhood. Remember to relax, breathe, and enjoy this passage into your evening. This is the perfect time to detach from the burdens of your job and observe the people and places along your path home. Let the sights and sounds quiet your mind. By the time you return home, you'll feel renewed and ready for whatever awaits you. ✳

enriching your home life

27

unlock serenity's door

Just when you thought you had left all of your troubles behind at work, your commute home can leave you all wound up again. Try this exercise while you're still standing at your front door with your keys in your hand.

① Take three breaths and begin to ground yourself in the present moment. Feel how it's a relief to be home. Your work is behind you now, and you're free to relax for the night.

② Select your door key and draw strength from the fact that this key has the power to unlock your freedom, ushering you into the awaiting comforts of your house or apartment.

③ Place the key into the lock and turn the key slowly. Move slowly and deliberately forward through your doorway, shedding the unhealthy layers of stress and leaving them outside to dissipate. Those negative thoughts and feelings are not welcome in your home.

④ As you close the door behind you, take a moment to say good-bye to those unwanted, clinging fears and uncertainties.

⑤ At last, serenity awaits you. ✳

28

arrive home together:
your body and your mind

Even as you return home, hurry, worry, and the momentum of the day can keep your attention far from your physical body or the present moment.

Try the following practice to help you arrive home united in body, mind, and spirit:

① As you approach your home, begin to pay attention mindfully.

② Notice how things look without coloring your observations with judgments or stories. Look at your neighborhood, your yard, your front door, or the outside walls of your apartment building, for example. See their color, shape, and texture.

③ Notice the sounds happening right now, in and around your home—soft sounds, loud sounds, pleasant ones, and even harsh ones.

④ Once you're inside, allow your mindful attention to connect you with what is present.

⑤ Walk mindfully through your home. Or alternatively, stand in one spot and open your attention, receiving all of the sights, sounds, and smells.

⑥ End with an acknowledgment, perhaps with gratitude, saying something like "I am home. May I connect deeply with this life." ✳

29

waterfall of the mind

When you return home from your workday, the first few minutes can be challenging. For example, maybe you have six unreturned phone messages, it's trash night, the kids are yanking on each leg for your immediate attention, and you still have to unpack the groceries and prepare dinner. You need a quick, mindful stress reduction exercise to help you get through the rest of your evening tasks in a calm and focused manner. Take the next several minutes to get grounded and to transition more smoothly from your workday.

This guided visualization will help you symbolically detach from work:

① Take five deep and relaxing breaths.

② While seated comfortably with your eyes closed, transport your mind and body to a peaceful lagoon with a gentle waterfall. From where you sit, you can see and hear the refreshing cascade of water showering over ancient rocks worn smooth over time.

③ You approach the waterfall and find the temperature is just to your liking.

④ As you stand beneath the falls, you feel the inner serenity that is washing over you, refreshing and renewing you from head to toe. ✳

(30

---

soulful cooking

In cultures across the globe, the preparation of each meal is of the greatest importance—from the placement of dishes, to infusing color with garnishes, to the complement of flavors. By taking more interest in the smaller details, you will consciously reconnect to the ritual of dinnertime.

In many ways, we are magicians in the kitchen, transforming a few vegetables into a delightful array of tastes and aromas. Whether you eat alone or with friends or family, handle each item for your meal and consider what's appetizing or healthy about it. Appreciate each one and feel gratitude for the incredible diversity of ingredients available to you. See how many colors you can incorporate into a meal, and experiment with new ways of cutting vegetables. Instead of listening to news or having the television on in the background while you cook, listen to soothing music so that you infuse the meal with peaceful good wishes.

Convey soulfulness and ritual into your cooking routine, and prepare your food with love and with special attention to presentation. Then pick out some lively cloth napkins, light a candle, and place fresh flowers or a photo of a loved one on the table. Allow your meal to nourish not just your body, but your spirit. ✳

31

where happiness lives

Foreground: what dominates your attention. Background: everything else.

When worries or stressful situations grow large and loud, they tend to dominate the foreground of your experience in every moment. A simple, mindful shift of focus from foreground to background can illuminate the many places where happiness still lives—even in distressing moments.

① Breathe or listen mindfully for about a minute.

② Set your intention. For example, "May this practice bring peace and balance to my life."

③ Breathe or listen mindfully. Name any worries or problems in the foreground of your awareness. Let them be.

④ Deliberately shift your attention from those worries to your background, to your surrounding environment. See, hear, and sense all that is around you.

⑤ Acknowledge and appreciate the sources of beauty and happiness around you: loved ones, pets, plants, beautiful objects—all of it.

⑥ Open to any feelings of joy and gratitude that begin to arise in you. ✳

32

still the mind

Never underestimate the value of small rituals for every-day household chores. You can bring mindful presence into doing the laundry, washing dishes, or making dinner. These small, routine ceremonies are opportunities to still your mind and give you a small breathing space within the hurly-burly of everyday life. The following exercise takes only five minutes and can be incorporated into any activity.

① Begin by focusing your attention on your breathing. The rhythm and cadence of each breath is what will help set your pace for your evening chores.

② Be mindful of every detail of your ritual. For example, if you're doing the laundry, are you separating the whites from the colors? Really see the colors: Are they faded or bright? Are there many colors or just a few? Feel the textures of the different fabrics. What does the laundry soap smell like? Do you use fabric softener? How does it smell? Are you a person who is concerned about biodegradable detergent? Consider all the places these clothes have gone. What memories and feelings do some of these garments hold for you or your family members? ✳

33

relax; you're home

Release the tensions of the day and refresh your body and mind by taking five good minutes to relax soon after arriving home.

① Choose a comfortable, quiet place to sit or lie down, someplace where you won't be interrupted.

② Breathe or listen mindfully for about a minute.

③ Set your intention. For example, "May I be more calm and relaxed through this practice."

④ Bring your attention to your body—all regions and parts, even the deep inner body.

⑤ Imagine that you're breathing in peace and ease, and that peace fills your entire body with each inhalation.

⑥ Imagine that you're breathing out all the toxins and stress of your workday with each exhalation.

⑦ When your mind wanders, don't view it as a mistake. Just gently return your attention to your breath.

⑧ End by opening your eyes and moving gently. ✳

34

bless me!

Before you wolf down your dinner, take a few minutes to express gratitude. We have a tendency to get so caught up in our mindless routine, our nagging hunger, and our rush to finish before our favorite sitcom that we overlook the many blessings that grace our lives. Take the time to acknowledge at least five things that you feel genuinely grateful for this evening. The act of feeling and expressing gratitude has a way of opening your perspective and shining light on the good things in your life, however small. Here are some ideas for the types of things your list might include:

- I'm grateful that it didn't rain today.

- My best friend called.

- I'm thankful to be in good health.

- There is abundant love in this world and enough for everyone.

- This meal is plentiful and delicious.

End your gratitude list with the words "This life is a miracle. There is magic and beauty to be found in every waking moment. Thank you for this life of bounty," or something similar. ✳

35

bite by savory bite

So often, we eat mindlessly while reading or watching television, or even while driving. Eating mindfully and with particular attention to the simple act of chewing can be a vital way of connecting more deeply with your body and your health. Conscious eating means putting aside all distractions and enjoying your meal with the full awareness of all your senses—sight, sound, smell, texture, and taste—and being aware of every movement you make. Try this exercise with your very first bite of food.

① Begin by taking three deep, relaxed breaths when you're seated before your meal.

② Take notice of the way you hold your eating utensils. Are you right-handed or left-handed?

③ What would you like your first bite to consist of? The salad? The main entrée? The side dish?

④ Observe how much food you have on your fork. Notice its shapes, textures, and colors.

⑤ Which aromas in this meal are most pleasing to you? What do they remind you of?

⑥ As you take this first bite into your body, eat slowly and methodically, chewing at least twenty times before you swallow.

⑦ Take the time to savor every bite and fully experience all of the taste sensations. ✳

36

don't wait to laugh

Laughter has many positive effects, including stimulating the heart and lungs and shifting us away from feelings of fear, isolation, and loneliness. And here's a secret about laughter: You don't have to wait for something funny to happen in order to laugh!

Give yourself a laughing break whenever you need one. This practice is one way to do so, but feel free to modify it or explore laughing however you like.

① Come into the present moment by breathing mindfully or listening mindfully for about a minute.

② When you're ready, let the first waves of laughter seep through you.

③ Make the sounds of laughing, letting them start deep inside.

④ You might begin with some soft tee-hees, a rolling ha-ha, or a deep ho-ho.

⑤ However you begin, laugh wholeheartedly, allowing the energy of laughing to take you wherever it will. Let the laughter grow until it takes over your body, giving in to shaking, stomping your feet, and waving your arms.

⑥ Have some fun! ✳

37

s.o.s.: message overload

Many of us are so dependent on our fast-paced, efficient new technology that we can hardly remember how we lived without these so-called essential items—voice mail, cell phones, e-mail, fax machines, and the like. But there was a time when people didn't have ten places to check their messages, a time when everyone had to rely on snail mail. Though we can't return to simpler times, we can find ways to reduce the level of stress that these technologies contribute. Take a few minutes each day to find ways to reduce the technological clutter. You may just free up extra hours every night for relaxation. Here are some useful suggestions to get you on your way:

- E-mail: Don't be afraid to reduce the number of e-mails you receive (even from friends and family). A short, simple e-mail announcement that you need people's help to reduce excessive hours spent on the computer will go a long way.

- E-mail: Delete all suspicious e-mail, spam, or other unwanted solicitations immediately.

- Voice mail and cell phone: Change your setup so that callers have only thirty seconds to leave a message (and change your outgoing message to alert them to this). ✳

38

time-out!

There are numerous distressing circumstances that can sabotage your tranquillity at home: your Visa bill, a pile of dirty dishes, or an empty refrigerator. Sometimes it doesn't take much before you hit your boiling point and even the sound of the phone ringing can spiral you into a bad mood. When you feel the first inklings of this pressure, you deserve a free time-out card.

The following exercise will help guide you to a place of stillness. Remember to maintain an awareness of the present moment by taking a few deep, diaphragmatic breaths and setting your intention.

① First, shut off your phone. Find a quiet place where you can sit or lie down comfortably.

② Begin this practice of calming your mind by saying something along these lines to yourself: "The messages can wait. The dishes can wait. The dog can wait. There will be time in the end to get to things that need to be done."

③ Say the following affirmation: "Through this practice, I am achieving greater comfort and calmness from deep within my mind and body. I am cultivating inward stillness."

④ This gentleness from within will infuse the rest of your night. ✳

39

give the gift of inner space

A habit of answering e-mails and phone calls daily can lead to an erosion of your sense of privacy, inner calm, and well-defined personal space. Soon after you arrive home and get settled, give yourself the gift of personal space and privacy by putting e-mails and phone calls on hold for a time.

Here's a practice to help you set aside personal time:

① Sit comfortably, and breathe or listen mindfully for about a minute.

② Set your intention. For example, "May this practice bring me greater peace and ease."

③ Offer yourself the gift of a specific period of time, whether just an hour or two or all evening. During that time, consciously let go of e-mail and let your voice mail answer any phone calls.

④ Notice your inner reactions to the gift of space and time. Acknowledge all the feelings that arise for you. You may feel relief, gratitude, or empowerment, or you may feel boredom, guilt, or worry. You can learn from any reaction, whether positive or negative.

⑤ Let the space and time you've given yourself, and the insights you gain from this gift, bring you peace and ease. ✳

40

first-aid kit

Chronic stress manifests differently, mentally and physically, for everyone, but a common outlet for most people is turning to unhealthy food choices. Or you may be so busy that you skip meals altogether. Despite what we know about fueling our bodies for optimal health, everyone has a breaking point and cannot resist indulging here and there—a scone for breakfast, free donuts at work, a piece of chocolate after lunch, or ice cream before bed. It's no wonder that so many people are enslaved by a sugar addiction. Take five minutes to plan ahead and pack a first-aid snack kit every day. Below are some quick, easy, and healthy snacks that will reduce your cravings for sugar, boost your energy level, and restore balance to your mood. The following foods can be eaten throughout the day or evening, but they're not meant to be substitutes for your regular meals.

- Cut up your favorite veggies and pack a dip, such as hummus.

- Celery sticks and peanut butter is always a tasty combo.

- Dried fruit, such as raisins, apricots, and cherries, is convenient to keep with you.

- Yogurt is a healthy snack that gives you energy, too.

- Apples with walnuts, almonds, or pumpkin seeds is a good treat. ✴

41

inhabit your kitchenscape

Hidden treasures live in the ordinary acts of daily life. Their riches can be discovered if you pay attention. Mindfully inhabit the landscape of your kitchen and remain aware throughout the cooking process. Doing so can uncover wonders!

① Approach your dinner preparation mindfully, anchoring your attention through mindful breathing or mindful listening as you begin and from time to time as you're cooking.

② Pay mindful attention to your "inner weather" along the way—any sense of hurry, worry, or whatever else you may feel.

③ As you proceed, take a mindful breath and acknowledge what you're doing—cutting vegetables or stirring a pot, for example.

④ Open yourself to all of the sensations, smells, and sounds in the kitchen: See the colors of different ingredients and watch how their colors change as they cook. Hear the sizzling as you add ingredients to a hot pan. Smell the aromas of herbs and spices and feel how comfortable your favorite knife is in your hands. Taste as you go, and consider how cooking changes ingredients in both taste and texture.

⑤ Move intentionally, bring kind attention to the task at hand, and rest in an inner spaciousness as you work. Being present, discover and enjoy! ✳

42

your worry basket

If you inherited the worry wart gene, then you're well versed in the mental ruminations that can plague a quiet night at home. You worry about the strange ticking noise that the car started making. You worry about an awkward conversation you had with your boss. You may find yourself on a hamster wheel of worries, running in circles but not making any forward progress at all.

The following practice will help you stop spinning your wheels and let go of those bothersome thoughts.

① Begin by making a mental or written list of all your worries, large or small, rational or far-fetched.

② Visualize or find a small wastepaper basket or box in which you can stash your worries.

③ Imagine tearing off each individual concern or fear and tossing it into your storage bin. If you've made a written list, go ahead and actually do this.

④ Say these words out loud: "I am letting go of these nagging thoughts. Some are important and some are not. But right now, I am reclaiming my right to enjoy life, live fully, and feel safe and secure tonight." ✳

43

the clutter patrol

Acluttered home can amplify any sense of feeling over-whelmed and magnify the stresses of the day. A few minutes focused on reducing your household clutter can go a long way toward diminishing your anxiety. Before you start your evening routine, take the next five minutes to straighten up and organize. Even a little tidying up will guarantee that you'll have a more pleasant evening, and hopefully a more tidy house to come home to tomorrow. You can't clean the whole house in five minutes, but a couple of minor adjustments will help restore your sense of ease and tranquillity:

- Toss all the extra magazines and newspapers lying around into your recycling bin.

- Empty the dish rack or dishwasher.

- Clear off the kitchen counters and dinner table and put away any stray items or leftovers.

- Toss any dirty clothes into the hamper.

- Collect all the scattered miscellaneous paper, coupons, and mail and stack them neatly in one pile on your desk. ✳

44

mindful dishwashing

What makes a chore a chore? Not wanting to do it? Wishing you were someplace else? Thinking there are more important things to do?

Attitudes like these tend to fuel habits of inattention and feelings of frustration. Explore the power of mindfulness —paying attention on purpose, as if it really mattered—to transform a chore into something interesting and enjoyable. In this practice, you'll do the dishes mindfully, but you can take this approach with other chores, as well.

① As you begin to wash, check your "inner weather." Acknowledge and allow any feelings or thoughts that are present—without judging yourself.

② As you're washing, pause occasionally and take a few mindful breaths.

③ Be attentive to the variety of experiences unfolding in the process of dishwashing. Notice all of the sensations you feel; for example, dampness, heat, coolness, or heaviness.

④ Open your awareness to sounds and smells as they arise. Also be mindful of your thoughts and feelings.

⑤ When your attention wanders or your mind starts speaking, be kind. Gently notice this has happened and return your attention to the total experience. ✳

45

sacred spaces

Most of us understand an altar to be a designated place or space where spiritual ceremonies are performed. For many people, their home is also a temple, a sanctuary from the burdens of outside pressures. Increasing numbers of people have created altars in their home for meditation or prayer, or simply as a place to display sacred objects. Altars can bring significant meaning and intention into your home life. Take a few minutes today to start the process of building your own personal altar. Here are some creative ideas to help get you started:

- Consider where you'd like to set up your altar—maybe in your garden, in the dining room or your bedroom, or on a bookshelf.

- Collect the items you'll need to create this sacred space—perhaps a small table, a beautiful piece of cloth, crystals, candles, incense, seashells, photos of loved ones, or any object of personal value or that elicits a meaningful memory.

- Reflect on what your altar represents to you. Is this where you come for grounding with yourself and the universe? Is this where you would like to pray? Or perhaps you come here to reconnect with the greater forces of nature. ✳

46

you are home; time to get dressed!

The clothes we wear in different situations often symbolize different aspects of ourselves. Let go of the busyness, hurry, and worry of the workday as you mindfully change clothes soon after returning home.

① As you begin the process of changing out of your work clothes, take a few mindful breaths and acknowledge that this is part of your transition to life at home.

② Set your intention, saying something like "May changing clothes more mindfully bring me into the present moment and give me freedom and joy."

③ Consciously acknowledge each action as you change clothes, staying as present as you can for what is happening. Here are some examples: "Now I am taking off my coat. Now I hang it up." "Now I take off my shoes. Now I put my shoes away." "Now I put on my sweater." "Now I put on my jeans."

④ Remember to take a mindful breath from time to time.

⑤ Finish by acknowledging that you are truly home. ✳

47

break the routine

The urge to collapse in front of the TV after dinner can become second nature and part of your evening routine. Unfortunately, TV can eat up your free time, and if you're not careful about what you're watching, you may end up watching anything and everything. Break your routine tonight and limit your television time. Make a mental or written list of more-rewarding options for how to spend your evening. Try to think of activities that may bring more long-term fulfillment and lasting enjoyment. Here are some suggestions to inspire and motivate you:

- Go for a leisurely walk or jog around your neighborhood.

- Write down your thoughts and feelings in a journal.

- Do something creative: paint, draw, play music, or do woodworking or other crafts.

- Take a hot bath.

- Meditate.

- Exercise.

- Read a book.

- Collect old clothes and other items to donate to a charity.

- Start a new project, such as organizing photos.

- Give yourself permission to just do nothing. ✳

48

wholesome fun

Have you ever been doing something fun only to realize afterward that your attention has been elsewhere? Take five good minutes to explore the power of paying attention on purpose in the midst of having fun. Let your *whole* self have some fun!

① Sit and breathe or listen mindfully for about a minute.

② Set your intention. For example, "May this practice awaken joy and ease in me."

③ Choose a favorite fun activity and start doing it.

④ For the next few minutes, open your awareness and attend to the experience as it unfolds and flows through all of your senses. Notice sensations, sounds, smells, and tastes; acknowledge your thoughts; and recognize and receive all the pleasant feelings that arise.

⑤ Paying attention on purpose without judgment, let the *whole* experience come to you through *all* of your senses.

⑥ Bring your attention back to your fun activity whenever your mind wanders, and do so without any judgments or critical thoughts. You have *not* made a mistake just because your attention wandered.

⑦ Inhabiting your whole being—your heart, mind, and body—be present for the fun! ✳

49

evening mishaps

When stress hijacks you in your home, it can hold you hostage for the rest of the evening. Stress can result from an argument with a loved one, unexpectedly high bills, your car breaking down, or your heart getting broken. On these nights, your only source of strength and understanding may lie in your ability to accept what's happened and let go of control (and the desire to control). In our hurried, chaotic lives, where we're usually juggling multiple tasks, we often delude ourselves with feelings of being in control. Nevertheless, most of us are keenly aware that there's so much we cannot control. The positive affirmations below may help you restore balance and compassion and accept what you cannot change. Remember to pay attention to your breath, inhaling strength and empathy and exhaling the will to be in command. Say any or all of the following affirmations aloud, or create your own:

- "The world won't end if I wait until morning to deal with this situation."

- "I don't have power over this situation and that is okay. I am learning to let go."

- "Today was difficult and I wish I could change my predicament. But tomorrow will be a new day to start over again. Tomorrow will bring hope and promise." ✳

☽ 50

---

between worlds

Your relationship to the outer world is a direct reflection of your inner world. If you're feeling angry, for example, you're likely to interact with the world around you in abrasive and uncaring ways. Or if you feel fearful, it's unlikely that you'll move in the world with confidence.

This practice invites you to explore how cultivating inner feelings of kindness might influence your relationship to the outer world.

136

① Sit comfortably either indoors or outdoors.

② Close your eyes and breathe or listen mindfully for about a minute.

③ Set your intention. For example, "May this practice help me open to awe and beauty in my life."

④ Breathe or listen mindfully a bit longer.

⑤ Open your eyes and look around attentively.

⑥ Imagine speaking kindly and with gratitude to whatever experience comes before you—to sights, sounds, sensations, all of it. Say "Thank you. May you be well. May you be safe."

⑦ Acknowledge your inner reactions. Continue to thank the world around you and wish it well.

⑧ End by sitting quietly. What do you feel? ✳

reconnecting with
yourself and others

51

say hello

W hen you arrive at home, in that moment when you first see your loved one (or loved ones), deliberately stop the rushing and momentum of your day and bring your attention to the present moment, and to those who are in front of you.

① Pay attention kindly and on purpose, making good eye contact with each of your loved ones.

② Breathing mindfully, allow each breath you take to bring you calm and ease, and to deepen your connection with what is happening now, in this moment.

③ Allow yourself to really see and acknowledge your loved ones. It may help to speak quietly to yourself, saying something like "This is my partner (or family), who loves and supports me" or "We are together again, and I know it won't always be this way."

④ Say hello with all of your heart. Speak to each one from your heart. Embrace each one with all of your heart.

⑤ Allow your heart to open to the preciousness of this moment. ✳

52

sensuality sparklers

Each of us has a sensual side. Despite how mainstream media or society may demonize it, our sexuality is a fundamental and natural part of our being; it's reflected in how we live our lives, how we build relationships, and how we create intimacy with others and ourselves. Though we may at times neglect or forget about our sensual needs, most of us have an undeniable craving and hunger for sensual experiences in our lives.

This next exercise is about discovering creative ways to tap into your sensuality and to radiate the kind of sensual energy that you most aspire to. Take a few quiet, reflective moments with yourself to make a mental or written list of what you would be willing to try to enhance your inner sensual vitality. Here are some ideas to get you started:

- Soothingly massage your body head to toe with a scented lotion. As you rub each area, give praise and appreciation to that part of your body for all the hard work it does for you.

- Compliment yourself on five areas of your body that make you unique and beautiful.

- Think back on a time when part of your body pleasantly surprised you or when someone complimented you about your body or your sensuality. ✳

53

have mercy

How do you usually respond to your inner feelings of pain and vulnerability? Many people meet inner pain with denial or rejection rather than kindness and compassion for themselves. If this is the case for you, this practice will help you explore how it feels to have mercy for yourself.

① Breathe or listen mindfully for about a minute.

② Set your intention. For example, "May this practice give me comfort and peace."

③ Breathe or listen mindfully for a few more breaths.

④ Recall some difficulty or pain in your life.

⑤ Open yourself and feel your distress as much as you safely can.

⑥ As a parent would hold their child, imagine holding yourself and your pain with kindness. Speak gently to yourself, saying something like "It's okay; I am okay" or "May I be safe and well." Or use whatever words will bring you comfort.

⑦ Repeat your phrase for as long as you like.

⑧ Keep it with you day and night. ✳

54

shoulders of loving-kindness

Some days more than others, you may feel bogged down by heartache or sadness. Depression is difficult to shake off easily without some help and support. Tonglen, a Buddhist practice, is a powerful visualization wherein one actually takes on the pain of the world. Knowing about the Tonglen practice—how others are taking on our pain—we can imagine this loving support and compassion present for ourselves at all times.

This exercise involves imagining the whole world shouldering some of your pain and suffering for a moment. Take these five minutes to imagine someone else providing the loving support and reassurance that you need right now. Around the globe, there is bountiful tenderness and compassion for all that you're going through—enough to go around for everyone. Tapping into a visualization of this expansive global support network will help you feel less alone and isolated. Use this imagery of a thousand gentle caretakers around the planet to lighten your load and bring a sense of comfort. ✳

55

deeper communication

Too often we communicate without being present: listening without really hearing and sometimes speaking without really thinking. Next time you're communicating with someone, by phone, e-mail, or text message, or in direct conversation, use the following practice to explore a deeper relationship:

① Breathe mindfully for a few breaths, bringing your focus to the other person.

② Relax, stop doing anything else, and really take in what the other person is communicating. Hear their words, the tones, the pauses. If their communication is in writing, really read every word.

③ As you listen or read, anchor yourself in the present moment with some mindful breaths now and then.

④ Notice how the tendency to compose an answer, argue, agree, or create stories in your mind all take attention away from what the other person is communicating to you. As best you can, let go of all that chatter. Just listen wholeheartedly.

⑤ When responding, devote the same level of attention and intention to your own communication. Don't just reel off a pat answer; offer a response that acknowledges and addresses what the other has said. Let your words come from deep within. You may be surprised. ✳

56

permission to cry

When was the last time you had a good cry? You might have teared up during a sentimental movie, after a breakup, or when remembering a sweeter time. Do you give yourself permission to cry and release? Or do you hold back your tears and feel bottled up? Despite the out-of-control feelings you may experience when you cry, doing so frees your mind and body from the constant need to be in control of your feelings. Crying can heal the soul, and children seem to know instinctively the benefits of a good cry. Sometimes the best remedy for your bucket of woes is to have yourself a good old-fashioned cry.

Take a few moments to reflect on the myriad of emotions that you've been suppressing throughout the day in order to maintain your job, relationships, and responsibilities. Release those emotions by giving yourself permission to blubber, sob, weep, complain, and wallow as much as you need to. After you've had a fair amount of time to lament your troubles, it's important to practice self-care—to be kind and compassionate, loving and gentle with yourself, as a parent would be for an upset child. Follow up with a hug, a cup of hot cocoa, a call to a supportive friend, or a soothing bath. ✳

57

appreciate someone

Stress and the hurry and worries of daily life can lead to feelings of separation and isolation even from those dearest to us. Kind attention is the key to restoring your sense of connection with loved ones. This practice will help you rekindle your appreciation for and connection to someone close to you.

① Before leaving work in the evening, take time to sit quietly.

② Breathe or listen mindfully for about a minute.

③ Set your intention. For example, "May this practice help me feel a deeper connection with _____ [say their name to yourself here]."

④ Bring the image of the named loved one into your heart and mind.

⑤ Reflect on how this person loves and supports you. Recall a specific act or some kind words.

⑥ Allow and acknowledge any feelings that arise, including love, appreciation, and gratitude.

⑦ When you next see your loved one, hold them close, mindfully, and say thank you. ✷

☾ 58

body mantra

Even when the workday is behind you, you may find that you experience all of your stored-up pain and muscle tension at the end of the day. While you have a sense of relief to be home, you may feel your neck stiffening or have shooting pains running up and down your back. The following self-hypnosis will guide you in visualizing your body's ability to reduce muscle strain and fatigue. You can do this visualization sitting or standing, whichever is more comfortable.

① Take a few slow and relaxing breaths before you begin.

② Scan your body to identify the places where you store your tension—feet, back, arms, shoulders, and so on.

③ Once you've located these specific areas, begin training your body to relax by saying, "I am sending peace and comfort throughout my body. When I am in a relaxed state of being, my body works inherently and instinctively to heal my aches and soreness."

④ As you begin to feel the release of tension in your body, reaffirm to yourself, "I will feel more alert and refreshed after this mindful practice." ✳

59

tune out the negative tape loop

The highway to relaxation doesn't come with a simple road map. The critical inner voice, anxious concerns, and an endless list of things undone can interfere with your ability to unwind. This next meditation is for liberating yourself from those mind traps so you can achieve a genuinely tranquil state of being.

① Find a comfortable place to sit, then slowly count back from the number ten, staying in tune with your circular breathing rhythm.

② Select a single word or phrase to correspond with each inhalation, and another for each exhalation. For example, with each inhalation you might think "patience," and with each exhalation, "perseverance." Or concentrate on "I am calm" as you inhale and "I am well" as you exhale.

③ As you breathe in and out, begin to concentrate on your corresponding words:

> "Calm" as you inhale,
>
> "Peace" as you exhale,
>
> "Calm" as you inhale,
>
> "Peace" as you exhale, and so on.

④ When your mind wanders, gently return to your words and breathing for focus.

⑤ As you come out of your meditation, be aware of your surroundings, the sights and sounds, and the easing of your mind and body. ✳

☾ 60

---

lend a helping hand

Doing for others is a beautiful way to connect, and to shift away from any inner feelings of isolation and upset. Experiment with the following practice. Not only will it benefit your loved one, it's also an avenue for your own self-discovery.

① Notice when someone needs help—doing dishes, laundry, homework, anything.

② Offer to help.

③ Breathe mindfully for a few breaths. Bring mindful attention to your inner life as you join in the task.

④ Acknowledge any inner resistance you feel. Speak kindly to this part. Say something like "I know you're upset. Don't worry; we will take care of you." Speak kindly to yourself.

⑤ Bring attention to the task itself. Be present as you work and pay attention on purpose to each detail.

⑥ Offer the work, your partner, and yourself a smile at times.

⑦ Let your mind and heart open and soften as you work. Feel the satisfaction that comes from helping your loved one. ✳

61

pools of kindness

The mind-body connection is well documented in medical science and by health practitioners. Tackle the stressors that lead to your aching muscles and frayed nerves with a holistic approach that speaks to all sides of yourself—physical, mental, emotional, and spiritual. When you practice compassion for yourself, you engage directly in an intimacy with all life on the planet and across the cosmos. When you're gentle and tender with yourself, you're practicing being gentle and tender with others and with the natural world around you. Try out the following mind-body visualization for healing.

① Sit in a comfortable position in a quiet room.

② Imagine a golden light surrounding you in a billowy cloud of reassurance.

③ See yourself being airlifted off a runway of frustration and sore muscles and being transported to a pool of water filled with kindhearted and caring warm currents that brush past your shoulders like minnows.

④ Your mental cleanse in this pool of kindness will wash away achy muscles and restore a smooth, supple feeling throughout your body.

⑤ As you return from this calming mind wash, you'll feel refreshed and open to receiving your family's needs and desires. ✳

62

the value of forgiveness

Whether we acknowledge it or not, we pay an enormous cost for unresolved anger, grudges, and grievances. What if baby steps toward forgiveness could open up your doors to healing and deepening your connections to yourself and your loved ones? Learning to forgive can help you release some of the emotional baggage that weighs you down like cumbersome sandbags. When you find pathways for forgiveness, you start changing how you respond to people who may not behave the way you want them to.

Unlocking forgiveness doesn't mean you condone the act that hurt you, nor does it require any confrontation or acknowledgment from anyone. Forgiveness is a mindful practice that starts from within your soul and will reverberate throughout your being. Begin by focusing on a specific situation or person that you'd like to forgive. Next, set your intentions by saying aloud, "I have the capacity to be a forgiving person. By forgiving, I am finding peace inside in order to be capable of love and trust again. Forgiveness is for me alone and will allow me to move forward with my life." ✳

63

what do *you* want to do?

Attention is a precious gift. Stopping, asking, and listening is a potent combination to connect with others—and with yourself. When you arrive home from work, try taking five good minutes to hear what a good friend—you—wants to do.

① Soon after arriving home, sit or lie down comfortably where you won't be disturbed.

② Breathe or listen mindfully for about a minute.

③ Set your intention. For example, "May this practice help me know myself better."

④   Breathe mindfully for a few more breaths, allowing feelings of calm and ease to come to you.

⑤   As you feel more relaxed and your attention becomes steadier, ask yourself something like "What would I really like to do tonight?" or "What would be really enjoyable tonight?"

⑥   Listen deeply for your answer. Honor it. Allow yourself to be surprised. Learn about yourself.

⑦   Enjoy! ✳

64

time for you and me

How many times have you said to yourself, "Where did my evening go?" Somewhere between six o'clock and bedtime—your time off to chill out alone, tend to a couple of projects, or just check in with your family or friends—was swallowed up into the vortex of lost time. If this scenario happens often enough, it can become routine, and you may feel cheated out of the quality time that you really need for nurturing the relationships that matter the most in your life, including your relationship with yourself. Since there will always be a multitude of responsibilities demanding your attention, you may need to make a special effort to give your relationships the care and devotion that they deserve.

This exercise is about setting aside five minutes to check in with yourself and a loved one and scheduling some quality time together.

① Take a moment to scan your address book for a friend whom you'd like to reconnect with, or you might ask your partner for a date.

② Arrange for a time to get together, and after you've done so, mark your calendar and express to the other person how important this date is for you.

③ Remind the other person about your date a day or two ahead of time. ✳

65

the compassionate heart

It's all too easy to fall into a constricted perspective driven by self-interest and fueled by feelings of isolation and worry, and this can happen without your realizing it. A potent remedy for such confinement is compassion, opening your heart to the pain someone else is feeling. This practice will help you explore compassion and discover how it may be an antidote to your own troubles.

① Breathe or listen mindfully for about a minute.

② Set your intention. For example, "May this practice soften my heart and give me joy."

③ Think of someone you know who is facing pain or difficulty.

④ Breathe or listen mindfully as you focus on them. Acknowledge their distress.

⑤ Imagine speaking kindly to them, as a loving parent would to an injured child, saying "May your pain be eased" or "May you find peace." Or express this in your own words.

⑥ Repeat your phrase quietly as long as you like.

⑦ End by becoming silent. Notice what you feel. ✳

66

write it out

You may not think of yourself as a writer or as someone who would keep a journal, but immeasurable emotional healing can come out of writing your thoughts and feelings down, either in a journal or on paper to be tossed out. Writing helps you articulate, clarify, and release pent-up emotions, and it can also give you a renewed perspective. When you don't find creative outlets for your stress, anger, sadness, or confusion, these stored-up sentiments fester inside and can lead to disease.

Take a couple of minutes to jot down exactly what thoughts are clawing at your mind and what feelings are distressing your heart. You are writing only for yourself, so take this opportunity to be as truthful and uncensored as you possibly can. Write from the gut. Write with the intention to set free your worrisome or upsetting thoughts. If it helps you write more freely, you can throw away, burn, or otherwise destroy what you've written. Doing so can also symbolize letting those troublesome thoughts go. ✳

67

your good neighbor

How often do you stop and acknowledge the importance of your neighbors in making your house a home? This practice invites you to take five good minutes and wish your neighbor well. When you next speak to your neighbor, let this practice inspire you.

① Breathe or listen mindfully for about a minute.

② Set your intention. For example, "May this practice deepen my connection with my neighbors."

③ Picture one of your neighbors or a group of your neighbors.

④ Breathe or listen mindfully. Recall how your neighbor supports you.

⑤ Imagine speaking to them in a friendly tone and wishing them well, saying "May you be safe and peaceful" or "May you be healthy and happy." Or use whatever words feel appropriate to you.

⑥ Repeat the phrases quietly and kindly to yourself for as long as you like.

⑦ End by sitting silently for a few breaths. ✳

☾ 68

---

an ounce of appreciation

One way to loosen stress's vise grip on your life is to soften to the beauty all around you, opening your heart and mind to the kindness and joy that other people and pets bring to your life. It's harder to stay frustrated and angry when you're busy focusing on the goodness that surrounds you.

This practice invites you to keep a running mental or written list of what you appreciate about your family, friends, and pets, and even yourself. Here are some ideas for the types of things your list might include:

- I am a strong and resilient person and have survived difficult times with dignity and grace.

- I'm lucky to have generous and caring people in my life.

- I'm grateful that my partner loves me despite my flaws and shortcomings.

- My best friend has a great sense of humor, which helps me to lighten up and laugh.

- My pet reminds me daily that I am loved and needed. ✳

☽ 69

---

never alone

In your next mindful breath, or through your next mindful moment, the world might reach out its hand to you. You need never feel alone if you can receive the unfolding gift of life. This practice will help you develop a sense of how you're an integral part of the whole of the universe.

① Breathe or listen mindfully for about a minute.

② Set your intention. For example, "May this practice deepen my sense of belonging and connection."

③ Breathe mindfully for a few more breaths.

④   Shift your attention to sounds.

⑤   Open to and receive all sounds directly, and mindfully. Focus on each sound's *vibration*, not names or stories you attach to the sounds. Include the space between sounds.

⑥   Imagine that the vibrations are reaching out to comfort you. Imagine that the universe itself is reaching out to you, in the totality of its richness and wholeness—kindly—through each sound vibration.

⑦   Enjoy the variety—loud, soft, harsh, peaceful, urgent, steady, happy, whatever. Feel the vibration. Let this deep vibration and interconnection with the universe enliven your heart, mind, and body.

⑧   Recognize how the universal energies are always flowing in and through you. You *cannot* fall out of the universe. ✳

☾ 70

take stock of your life

If you are to truly practice living a life of purpose, intention, and gratitude, then you need to take inventory of every conceivable aspect of your life—material, emotional, mental, and spiritual. There's no time like the present to take stock and appraise the contents of your life in terms of their value to you. Ask yourself the following questions to help you get started on your path toward a life of greater meaning, focus, integrity, and appreciation:

- Do my belongings, attitudes, goals, obligations, commitments, relationships, habits, dreams, and wardrobe reflect my values?

- Do they fit my current lifestyle?

- Do they continue to serve me or give me pleasure?

- In what ways do they drain my energy, hinder my happiness, or otherwise not serve me well?

- What are some small changes or adjustments I could make this week to begin the process of weeding out the things that slow me down or diminish my quality of life? ✳

71

only this

Relationships are complex. We give and take, please and annoy, satisfy and disappoint. However, a loving relationship shouldn't require bartering. Perhaps being present with kind and compassionate attention is more what love is about.

What if you didn't always have to "do it right" or get what you "need"? What if you were to drop those stories for even a short five minutes?

① Breathe or listen mindfully for about a minute.

② Set your intention. For example, "May this practice enrich my relationship."

③ Breathe or listen mindfully for a few more breaths.

④ Focus on an important relationship, and specifically on the other person.

⑤ Ask this question: "What do I expect from you?" Listen for the answer.

⑥ Ask another question: "What if I expected or asked nothing from you?" Listen for that answer. Acknowledge and honor all of the responses.

⑦ What do you feel and notice? ✳

72

lower your standards

If you set high standards for yourself in regard to fulfilling the needs of others, then "no" can be the hardest word in your vocabulary to verbalize. You may suffer from feelings of terrible guilt or anxiety when yet another everyday obligation leaps into your path. It takes tremendous determination and practice to relax your standards. But learning to say no may save your life; it may rescue you from the unceasing clutches of a life overburdened with too many obligations, extra side projects, invitations, and unnecessary deadlines that steal away your precious energy and time.

Take a few moments to exercise your freedom to say no to things that zap your energy. Saying no will bolster your self-respect and your ability to put your needs first. Remind yourself that it's never too late to call someone back and say, "Something unexpected came up and I can't make it. Thanks for thinking of me." Or you might say, "Thanks for the invitation, but it conflicts with other plans." This is true: those "other" plans are for taking care of you. ✳

☾ 73

the pet who loves you

With a bark, a purr, a bounce, a wiggle, or a moving tail, your pet lets you know how happy they are to see you. Try taking five good minutes to really be with your loving friend.

① Engaging with your pet, pay attention mindfully to what's happening.

② Let yourself receive the experience as it unfolds, noticing your inner sense of joy, love, excitement, or anything else you may feel.

③ Notice the way your pet moves, hear the sounds they make, feel the texture of their fur, gaze at their face and into their eyes.

④ Open to the give-and-take and be present for your own speaking and playing. Breathe and listen mindfully if it helps you stay present and connected.

⑤ If your attention wanders or judgments arise, kindly notice what's happened and bring your attention back to your pet.

⑥ Allow yourself to receive the gifts of love, companionship, and belonging. ✳

74

optimism breather

As workload pressures build, you may feel frustrated, irritated, angry, or resigned. At times you may even convince yourself that your boss, coworkers, family, and friends don't care and don't want to help. Though it's natural to have these negative thoughts when you're tired and frustrated, it can wreak havoc in your personal relationships. You can begin to reduce this tension before you take it out on the ones you love by taking an optimism breather. Take the next five minutes to follow these simple steps to serenity:

① When stressful times flare up, at work or at home, find a place to sit quietly in a chair with your back resting comfortably.

② If you can, shut your door, turn off your cell phone, and close your eyes.

③ Take several diaphragmatic breaths.

④ Now think back on a time when you felt deeply happy, when you were laughing with contentment or love was fluttering throughout your body. Let this feeling of joy encircle you.

⑤ Allow this feeling of lightness and hope to form a smile on your face. Visualize this smile melting away your stress and helping you restore a sense of ease and clarity as you go about your business. ✷

75

just listen

Perhaps the most valuable gift we can offer another is our wholehearted attention. Unfortunately, when in conversation we often pay more attention to our inner response than to the actual words of the other. To counter this tendency, try the following experiment in mindful listening. Throughout this practice, use mindful breathing to stay focused and present.

① The next time you're in a conversation, breathe mindfully for a few breaths.

② Remind yourself that you are experimenting with mindful listening.

③ As the other speaks, bring attention to them and just listen. Let go of your own reactions, your inner reply or argument, and even efforts to please or show interest.

④ When your mind wanders, breathe mindfully to steady your focus.

⑤ Notice any thoughts of your own without becoming diverted by them; instead, breathe mindfully, and just listen.

⑥ Maintain your kind, spacious attention during times of silence, inviting the other person to share anything else they need to say. ✳

preparing for a good
night's rest

76

heed the call of a tired body and a weary mind

At some point in the evening, you may notice you feel tired and dull in mind and body. If you wonder "Am I tired?" or "Should I go to bed?" try taking five good minutes to connect with your body, heart, and mind.

① Kindly practice mindful breathing or listening for about a minute.

② Gently shift your attention to your mind, heart, and body. Allow all sensations and experiences to come to you, receiving them as you pay attention.

③ Notice sensations in your tired body: heaviness in your limbs, sinking eyelids, or low energy, for example.

④ Notice whether your mental alertness is diminished; for example, note any difficulty concentrating or a feeling of dullness.

⑤ Extend your awareness to your emotions. Do you have any feelings of upset, irritation, or even resistance to going to sleep? Name them kindly, acknowledging their presence.

⑥ Learn to recognize the call of your tired body and weary mind, then offer them relief. ✶

77

relaxing mind tonic

After a hectic day of work, errands, and responsibilities, getting a good night's sleep might seem like attempting to stop a fast-moving train on a downhill slope without brakes. Thoughts and tasks for tomorrow's agenda may be spinning and swirling in your mind with no hope for rest in sight.

Tonight, before you head off to bed, take a couple of minutes to make a cup of calming herbal tea, such as chamomile or peppermint. (Some herbal teas can be stimulating, so choose wisely or seek advice if you're uncertain.) Even if you don't have a taste for the tea, the ritual of preparing it is part of the passage of calming your nerves. During this process, take notice of every detail: What mug did you select? How does the tea smell, even before you brew it? Notice the sound of the kettle filling with water, the feel of its weight in your hand, the hissing of water drops dissipating on the stove, the heat emanating from the kettle, the boiling water splashing into your cup, the tendrils of white steam rising from your tea, and the calming aromatic fragrance. ✳

78

release this day

While lying in bed and waiting for sleep, if you pay attention to your heart, mind, and body, you may notice patterns of holding onto the events of your day, perhaps even resistance to letting go of them. This can interfere with a good night's sleep. Try taking five good minutes to consciously release your day.

① Breathe or listen mindfully for about a minute.

② Set your intention. For example, "May I release this day and welcome peace and calm within."

③ Imagine that your breath moves through all parts of you—your heart (emotions), mind, and body. As your breath moves naturally in and out, imagine that it brings calm and ease and carries away restlessness, stress, and upset.

④ Try speaking kindly to any particular part of you that's in distress, whether physical, emotional, or mental. Say something like "Thank you for all you do; you can rest now. You are released."

⑤ Try speaking to yourself kindly, saying something like "May the highest good come from all my actions today. I release them, and myself. May I be at peace."

⑥ End by breathing or listening mindfully for a few more breaths. ✳

◗79

---

tension buster

As you go through your day, you may store stress and tension in your body without being aware of doing so, and without knowing where you store it. The goal of the following practice, a full-body scan, is to reconnect you with where your body may be stockpiling your tension and to flood that area with intentional relaxation. As you do the exercise below, you'll probably feel your stored-up tension when you direct your focus to that part of your body. Another signal that you've got tension in an area is if you feel tight or sore when you are focused on a particular area.

① Lying in bed on your back with your eyes closed, breathe mindfully for one full minute.

② Now concentrate on the soles of your feet. Consciously tighten the muscles of your feet for a few seconds, holding tight, and then release.

③ Concentrate on your stomach muscles. Consciously tighten the muscles of your stomach for a few seconds, holding tight, and then release.

④ Concentrate on the muscles of your face. Consciously tighten the muscles of your face for a few seconds, holding tight, and then release.

⑤ Repeat this process of tightening the muscles in particular areas—your neck, back, legs, and so on—where you might be holding your tension, and then releasing.

⑥ Continue your mindful breathing as you relax into a peaceful sleep. ✳

80

finish your business

When difficult situations remain unresolved, it can impact your ability to relax and get a good night's sleep. Try to recognize when you're feeling particularly stuck or are struggling with something, someone, or some event from your day. This could be a good time to take five good minutes to deal with unfinished business.

① Breathe or listen mindfully for about a minute.

② Set your intention. For example, "May this practice help me find peace."

③ Breathe or listen mindfully for a bit longer.

④ Turn your attention to whatever is disturbing you. Give it a name: my health problem, my relationship, or my work situation, for example.

⑤ Breathe mindfully and gently ask, "What is needed for peace in this situation?" Listen patiently for any answer that comes. Listen deeply and without judgment. The answer may be a single word, or it may be an image or a sound. Ask your question again if it helps.

⑥ If you get no meaningful answer, notice that. Recognize that some things take more time than others. Acknowledge that you have asked, and affirm that you'll revisit the question as often as you need to. Let it all be for now. ✳

(81

---

stop this racehorse,
I want to get off

Why is it that no matter how dog tired we are, our emotions can keep us up half the night? The litany of "why me?" questions can riddle your tender heart and make you feel isolated and alone. Bedtime may be the hour when all your fears and uncertainties creep back in and agonize you endlessly. Take a few moments to follow this practice for emotional release:

① Begin by unbolting the floodgate for all your worries and fears, hurt feelings and disappointments. That's right, give them free rein on the racetrack of your mind for a full minute.

② Now focus on a particular emotion, such as loneliness, and create a verbal formula for helping you bring that feeling to a standstill. You may find it visually helpful to imagine your thoughts and feelings as horses and that you have the power to pull on the reins and bring them to a halt.

③ Say aloud, "My loneliness [or other emotion] is a part of what keeps my heart beating strong, but tonight I am getting off that ride. I am putting my emptiness to sleep."

④ Continue with your other emotions, saying "Tonight I am bringing my feelings of _____ to a stop. I am putting this emotion to rest." ✳

☾ 82

---

staircase to sleepy-town

Few things are worse than the agony of tossing and turning and ultimately finding yourself unable to sleep. Read through the following brief self-hypnosis script and then put it into practice to begin easing your way into a good night's rest.

① Close your eyes and follow the pace of your breathing mindfully to center you in the present.

② Ease your mind by saying, "I am feeling my body growing heavier and heavier, loosening and relaxing with each breath. I am feeling my mind evaporating into the clouds." Or you might repeat these words to yourself: "drowsy, comfortable, relaxed, at ease."

③ Now visualize a staircase that leads down to a place that calms you. With each step, you will become gradually more comfortable and more serene. Every step takes you deeper into complete tranquillity.

④ Take a moment to imagine your mind and body floating above the staircase, weightless, unbound, and unfettered. You will begin feeling the sensation of drifting deeper and deeper, feeling more and more drowsy, spiraling downward into total relaxation. ✳

83

feel gratitude for this day

Restful sleep is promoted by feelings of well-being and ease at bedtime. Unfortunately, your mind may often habitually dwell on negative or worrisome topics just when rest is near.

This simple practice of gratitude can help shift your experience from worry to ease.

① Lying in bed, breathe or listen mindfully for about a minute.

② Set your intention. For example, "May this practice free my heart and mind for restful sleep."

③ Breathe or listen mindfully for a few more breaths.

④ Recall and reflect on one good thing that happened or came to you this day. Relax, take some time, and open deeply to the experience. Feel the good wishes, the support, and the security that you received from this gift.

⑤ If you become aware of more things you're grateful for, feel their goodness deeply, too.

⑥ Let go of any critical judgments, comments, or stories about the things you're grateful for.

⑦ Rest in the goodness and say thank you. ✳

84

star-filled nights

When was the last time you stood outside beneath the stars? Even if you live in a city where you can't see them or at times when fog or clouds block your view, you know with absolute certainty that you're standing under the magnificent array of stars that stretch across the universe.

Let yourself spend a few minutes stargazing tonight, experiencing the sensations that only a sunset or moonbeams can bring to your mind, body, and spirit. Take notice of the stillness in the air, the chill against your skin, the chorus of crickets, the sweet scent of honeysuckle, and the quieting of life all around you. Imagine all the people tucked away safely in their beds, snuggled beneath warm blankets, and drifting off to sleep. Imagine all the dreams that are encircling their unconscious minds, transporting them in time shuttles to distant places, strange lands, and stranger stories. Soon, you'll be there too. ✳

85

fire, earth, water, air

You've taken care of everyone's needs: dinner is over, the kids are tucked in, the chores are done, and the cat is fed. You made sure everyone else is nourished, safe, and loved, but what about you? Perhaps it's been this way for so long that you don't even know what your needs are anymore. This grounding exercise will support you in connecting with your true inner needs and desires.

① Start with your breathing. As you inhale, acknowledge that others are cared for and secure; as you exhale, acknowledge that now it's time to take care of you.

② Visualize the four elements of nature that we cannot exist without and that ground us to this planet: fire, earth, water, and air. Empty your mind and imagine the room is filled with candlelight, bathing you in its warmth and glow. Even as you're carried along with the earth's rotation, you remain firmly rooted to the ground. Let the cool, crystal blue waters of calm wash over you and carry your burdens downstream. With every breath, your lungs fill with the life-giving forces of air.

③ In this meditative space, allow your needs and desires to surface. Honor and acknowledge them. ✳

86

say good night to your mind

Have you ever noticed that your mind often doesn't seem to know when your body is trying to sleep? It may help to treat a busy mind like a restless child at bedtime. As you're lying in bed, try this practice:

① Breathe or listen mindfully for about a minute.

② Set your intention. For example, "May I treat my busy mind with the kindness and patience of a loving parent."

③ Gently bring your attention to the thoughts and images buzzing in your mind.

④ Speak gently and quietly to your busy mind, as if speaking to a restless or worried child, saying something along these lines: "Thank you for all you do. It's time to rest now. You can play tomorrow. Time to sleep. Good night."

⑤ Breathe mindfully, allowing yourself to relax.

⑥ You may have to visit your busy mind a few more times. Always speak kindly, as if speaking to a child. ✳

87

bedtime rituals

If kids can have bedtime rituals, why can't you? Tonight, be mindful of your bedtime routine and be fully present in each moment-to-moment ritual. Take extra care in brushing your teeth, washing your face, drying your hands, changing into your comfy pajamas, pulling back the blankets, fluffing your favorite pillow, and hugging yourself good night.

Before turning out the lights, read yourself a bedtime story or try to remember one that was told to you when you were a child. Sing yourself a lullaby or a song that you remember from when you were young. When you were little, you likely did silly things to keep the nightmares and scary monsters away. Take five minutes to close your closet door, sneak a flashlight beneath your covers, and retell that bedtime story to yourself or your partner. Think about what or who made you feel safe when you were young. Consider what you could do for yourself tonight to feel protected and secure. ✷

88

your precious life

Your ability to sleep can be hijacked by stress from the day or memories of difficult situations. If you begin to feel isolated, overwhelmed, or vulnerable, this can further interfere with restful sleep. Spending a few minutes reflecting on a larger view of your life can help to restore peace and calm as you prepare for sleep.

① Shortly before or after going to bed, breathe or listen mindfully for about a minute.

② Acknowledge this day as one of many days in a month, a year, and over the years of your lifetime.

③ Recall that you have had many days—good and bad; many relationships—pleasing and painful; many experiences—pleasant and unpleasant.

④ Breathe mindfully.

⑤ Allow yourself to feel deeply the fullness and the richness of your life, remembering that life is made of much more than just one day or one event.

⑥ Can you feel gratitude for the variety and preciousness of your life? ✳

☾89

media vacation

As if it's not enough that we spend our days inundated by a constant barrage of sound pollution—car horns, shrieking sirens, people talking, planes overhead, incessant phone calls—how many of us spend our evenings with the TV blasting in one room, the radio blaring down the hall, the phone ringing off the hook, and the neighbor's dog barking all night long?

For the next five minutes, declare that no one in the house will turn on the television, computer, or stereo. While you're at it, go ahead and unplug the phone. Take the bold and courageous steps to temporarily disconnect. You need and deserve at least five solid minutes of absolute silence—no arguments, no gossip, not a murmur or a whisper from anyone for a whole five silent, sacred minutes of reprieve. (Hugging, kissing, and smiling are encouraged!) ✳

☾ 90

---

wish yourself a good night's rest

Being kind to others often comes easily. Being kind to yourself can, unfortunately, be more difficult. Bedtime is a good time to practice kindness to yourself. Try wishing yourself a good night's sleep just as you would wish the same to a loved one or a child.

①   As you're lying in bed awaiting sleep, breathe or listen mindfully for about a minute.

②   Set your intention. For example, "May this practice help me rest well."

③ Breathe mindfully for a few more breaths, allowing ease and relaxation to come to you.

④ Place one or both hands on your chest, over your heart.

⑤ Connect with feelings of kindness or friendliness within, such as the feelings you hold for a loved one or a dear friend.

⑥ Speak kindly to yourself, as if speaking to that loved one, and wish yourself a good night's rest. For example, tell yourself, "Sleep well," "May I rest deeply and well," or "Pleasant dreams, my friend."

⑦ Allow peace, ease, and relaxation to come to you.

⑧ Good night. ✳

91

spiritual force

After a long, arduous day filled with responsibilities and demands, bedtime can be an opportunity to get in touch with your spiritual side. Whether you consider yourself religious or not, you've undoubtedly pondered the mysteries of life. When you open yourself to the unknown workings of the universe, you are taking the time to acknowledge your purpose and meaning on the planet.

As you tuck yourself beneath the covers tonight, take a few minutes to step outside the clutter of your daily routine and its never-ending details and explore the depths of what is sacred in your life. As you settle into a relaxed breathing pattern, contemplate the perfection of the forces that have brought you to this time and place and granted you your unique life, with all its richness and complexity. Consider that this miracle of existence repeats itself endlessly through time and space. Contemplate the following questions as a means of guiding your mind, body, and spirit toward this infinite journey of the soul:

- Who am I? Why am I here?

- How am I a part of what is beautiful and miraculous on this planet?

- What experiences or activities make me feel connected to life outside myself? ✳

92

time to rest

The key to this practice is to *not* try to make anything happen! It is good enough to soften and to receive the experiences that come to you.

① Lying comfortably in bed, breathe or listen mindfully for about a minute.

② Set your intention. For example, "May I receive the gifts of ease and relaxation in body, mind, and heart."

③ Bring your attention to the physical sensations of your body. Speak to your body kindly, for example, saying "Thank you for all you did today. You may rest now."

④ Breathe or listen mindfully for a few breaths.

⑤ Bring attention to your heart and mind. If there is busyness or distress, speak kindly, saying, for example, "You have done enough today. Time to rest."

⑥ Continue to breathe or listen mindfully, and to speak kindly to your body, mind, and heart.

⑦ End by letting it all go. ✳

93

mental holiday

On the nights when your stress and worries creep into your bed, you need a quick and easy escape route. Take the next five minutes to visualize your perfect vacation. Imagine a getaway that brings you limitless serenity and calm, a place such as a beach, a forest, or a river. Once you've thought of your special place, take notice of what it is about this environment that makes it calm and relaxing.

- Is it the endless sound of waves washing on the shore? Is it the wind rustling through the trees? Is it the sound of flowing water, or is it perhaps the silence—the absence of the sounds of civilization?

- Is it the warmth of the sun on your shoulders or the feel of warm sand beneath your feet? Is it the smell of freshly mown grass or the crisp scent of autumn in the air?

- Are you lying in a hammock or sitting under a tree? Are you reading a book, watching a sunset, or just doing nothing?

- Are you caught up in the lush beauty that surrounds you or are you engulfed in the silent moment and the utter stillness of life itself?

Carry this calming imagery with you as you drift into sleep. ✳

94

good night, my friend

Feeling a sense of connection and belonging is not only a great source of support and well-being, it can also support a good night's sleep. This practice invites you to acknowledge and rest in the benefits of an important connection in your life.

① Shortly before or after going to bed, breathe or listen mindfully for about a minute.

② Set your intention. For example, "May this practice bring me ease and rest."

③ Think of a good friend. Picture that person as clearly as you can. Let yourself feel the warmth and support of their friendship.

④ Imagine you're speaking to your friend. Wish them well, using phrases like "May you be safe and protected," "May you be filled with joy," or any other words you like.

⑤ Repeat your phrase quietly for as long as you like.

⑥ End by saying good night to your friend. ✳

95

empty your mind

Each of us lugs around a wide array of emotions, troubling thoughts, and painful feelings that can be road-blocks—detours that get in the way of uninterrupted sleep. Luckily, the most basic of actions, breathing, is a powerful compass for navigating your mind, body, and spirit toward a path of inner calm. Tonight, prop yourself up on comfy pillows in your bed and give yourself a few moments to follow this simple meditation to clear your mind and restore inner harmony.

① First, envision your body drifting slowly upward like a kite. Feel the wind sweeping you up into a timeless continuum.

② As you inhale, you are breathing in hope and all things good and positive. You are absorbing the exquisite beauty of the skyline and expanding your potential to experience a free, unfettered life.

③ As you exhale, you are breathing out bad energy, negativity, and despair.

④ With each breath you feel lighter and more at ease. ✳

96

cultivate inner peace

For scores of centuries, Taoist practice has observed morning and evening prayers with the belief that evening rites can relax your soul, revitalize your energy, and improve your sleep. Through these daily prayers and meditations, Taoist masters cultivate inner peace with the self and outer peace with the whole world. Take time tonight to say your prayers, to give thanks for your daily blessings, to be open to the adventures that await you, and to nurture peace within yourself.

① While sitting in your bedroom and breathing mindfully and restfully, place both your hands over your heart.

② Say aloud, "Tonight I am following in the footsteps of ancient wise ones. With each breath, I am restoring inner and outer peace, in my heart and in the world."

③ In these quiet moments, you are freeing yourself from the negative thoughts and feelings that are obstructing your well-being.

④ Say aloud, "I am cultivating lasting wellness within myself. I am extending this goodwill beyond the limits of my body, so that it will permeate throughout the world." ✳

(97

---

ecstasy infusion

While you're preparing for bed, think of a time, either from your past or more recently, when you were really happy, when the feeling of joy, laughter, and pleasure infused your every step. Though the occasion has passed, you can re-create permanent happiness from this memory.

① Once you have a vivid, joyful moment in mind, comb your mind for details: Were you alone or with someone special? Were you at a park, out to lunch, or at home? What made the recollection special and happy?

② You can be a conduit for that bubbly feeling of contentment. Let it percolate throughout your whole body. Visualize holding this special memory in times of sadness, discouragement, or heartache.

③ Let your blissful remembrance be your guide to finding your way back to keeping a smile on your face and a soft glow in your heart. ✳

98

befriend yourself

Feelings of ease and peace, including a sense of safety, are wonderful allies for restful sleep. These feelings flow from your deep capacity for kindness and acceptance. It's important to remember that no matter what may happen in the outer world, you can always offer yourself those gifts of kindness and acceptance.

This practice can help you remember how to befriend yourself, and in so doing, to foster warm feelings of well-being that can help ease you into sleep.

① Breathe or listen mindfully for about a minute.

② Set your intention. For example, "May this practice bring me peace and a good night's sleep."

③ Breathe or listen mindfully for a few more breaths.

④ Imagine speaking quietly to yourself, as you would speak to a dear friend, with kindness and acceptance.

⑤ Wish yourself well, using words or phrases that speak to you on a deep level. For example, you might say, "May I be safe and filled with peace," "May I be happy and at ease," or "May I be healed and healthy."

⑥ Repeat this phrase for as long as you like.

⑦ End by resting quietly in silence. ✳

☾ 99

---

vision quest

Since time immemorial, cultures the world over have used the vision quest as a central rite of passage. A vision quest is a period of solitude wherein you seek inner revelation—a vision to steer your life in a direction of profound meaning and purpose. This vision quest exercise will bring you a sense of meaning or direction, as well as a sense of calm and inner stillness. The essence of this practice is to be mindful of the journey alone, not the goal or destination. You may reach the top of the mountain, or you may decide to sit down along the way and enjoy the vista. Your vision quest will take you to where you were meant to go and a restful sleep will await you there.

① Sitting or lying still, close your eyes and let go of any clinging details of your day. Your journey is one of the mind and spirit; no luggage needed.

② Begin visualizing your wide, open path at the base of a sacred mountain. As you begin your ascent mindfully, all is quiet and still, full of light and tranquillity. Each step propels you forward, sure-footed and full of conviction.

③ Pay attention to your feet, your breathing, and the world around you. Along the way, remain open to receiving messages, symbols, and signs. Your quest for greater truth and direction may take the shape of a word, an animal, or a sacred image.

④ You are traveling lightly and moving with ease. ✳

(100

the web of life

A good night's sleep is nurtured by feelings of belonging and connectedness. Gentle acts of attention and kindness at bedtime are potent reminders of your place in the web of life, and can also help you get the rest you need.

① Just before or after going to bed, breathe or listen mindfully for about a minute.

② Set your intention. For example, "May this practice bring me joy and comfort."

③ Breathe or listen mindfully for a few more breaths.

④ Picture the whole earth, as seen from space, or picture a region that you especially like.

⑤ Look closer, seeing all the forms of life there.

⑥ Open to and rest in your feelings of affection for those life-forms.

⑦ Wish them well, quietly saying phrases like "May you be safe and protected" or "May you be happy." Or use whatever words are most meaningful to you.

⑧ Practice as long as you like. ✳

Jeffrey Brantley, MD, is a consulting associate in the Duke Department of Psychiatry and the founder and director of the Mindfulness-Based Stress Reduction Program at Duke University's Center for Integrative Medicine. He has represented the Duke MBSR program in numerous radio, television, and print interviews. He is the best-selling author of *Calming Your Anxious Mind* and coauthor of *Five Good Minutes: 100 Morning Practices to Help You Stay Calm and Focused All Day Long*.

Wendy Millstine, NC, is a freelance writer and certified holistic nutrition consultant who specializes in diet and stress reduction. She is coauthor of *Five Good Minutes: 100 Morning Practices to Help You Stay Calm and Focused All Day Long*.

www.fivegoodminutes.com